Stray

By Suzanne DiTommaso

Stray: to travel along a route that was not originally intended; to be separated from the group; to be lost or have no home.

Always love again.
Suzanne DiTommaso

ISBN: 0998215414

PROLOGUE

A field in Wethersfield, Ohio
Early Spring 2002

The sun hung low in the sky and the clouds were pink and orange as the day was ending. A chilly breeze blew and nightfall was looming. Teems of early spring crickets and other buzzing insects filled the air with a constant hum and an old Chevy pick-up truck rattled down the road, tailpipe clanging. The old green truck with a rusted bumper, one blue door and no rearview mirror belched black smoke from the tailpipe. The long grass fanned in waves as the truck emerged at the top of the hill after passing the only two driveways on the old road. The truck blew up some dust as it came to a halt at the side of the road.

An old man wearing a black stocking cap and flannel shirt sat in the cab of the truck and looked in his rusty side view mirror. A car approached and slowed to a crawl. The man reached out the window and waved the driver on. He gave an obligatory friendly nod to the family in the car as they passed, and he watched as the vehicle disappeared out of sight. He peered at his side view mirror and listened very carefully. Once he was certain there was no one coming he forced open the door. The door made a loud clank as the window entombed in the door banged back and forth against the steel.

The man reached into the cab of the truck and pulled out a scrappy, gangly, collie/shepherd puppy. He looked from side to side as he held the dog, its legs dangling. The man reached down and pulled the loop of rope off the puppy's neck. The little dog's big brown eyes looked up at the man and then out across the field. The man could feel the puppy's heart beating. In complete silence the man in the stocking cap bent down and set the little dog on the side of the road. The dog sat, slightly slouching off the side of the road and looked up at the truck as the man got in and slammed the door. The gears ground as the truck pulled out onto the road. A cloud of exhaust smoke billowed out of the tailpipe and over the puppy as the truck's tires screeched. The puppy closed his eyes feeling the noxious fumes hit his tender little features. The smoke made him sneeze a tiny puppy sneeze. His eyes watered as he tried to open them, and when he did the old pick-up truck and the old man in the stocking cap were gone.

CHAPTER ONE

Struthers, Ohio
Spring 2015

It was a chilly afternoon in March and Katie Thompson sat quietly on the school bus as it made its way through her home town of Struthers, Ohio. Katie was small for her age with long light red hair and big green eyes. Katie was not exactly shy but she was also not a very sociable young girl. She was quite happy to be on her own and in her own thoughts as the chatter continued around her. The bus pulled up to the intersection of Second and Walnut and a dozen children stood up as the bus lurched to a halt with a loud swoosh of air from the airbrakes.

"Wait for the bus to come to a complete stop," the bus driver shouted, as she had done a thousand times.

Katie hoisted her back pack onto her shoulder and quietly filed out at the end of the line of children. She hopped off the last step and onto the pavement and slowly wandered along to the sidewalk as if she had nowhere to be. Well, actually she did have nowhere to be. Her mother wouldn't be home for another hour or so, and her father would not be home until much later. Katie was basically an only child. She had an older sister but she was eight years older than Katie and had gone off to college several years earlier. Now that Katie had turned twelve and started middle school she had finally convinced her mother she could stay home alone for that one hour gap. She hated that afterschool program but she was pretty bored after school.

Katie ambled down Walnut Street gazing at the new buds on the trees. The air was cold but not so cold that it made her hurry like it did in those winter days in Ohio that meant she had to be bundled up to her eyeballs. Spring was definitely in the air, and Katie was relieved to be wearing her new blue spring jacket and pink tennis shoes rather than her heavy coat and snow boots. When the snow was deep Katie had to follow the snow shoveled paths around the block to reach her house on Oakwood Drive, but since there was no snow today, she turned off the sidewalk to take the short cut. She hadn't used this route since the fall, and she could just make out the slightly worn path that would lead her through the backyards, a small wooded area and past the old shed finally bringing her out on Oakwood just two houses down from her own. Katie hummed as she moseyed through the first section and ran her hand along a rusty chain-link fence as the old shed came into view. Every year it looked a little more worn and a little less like it would make it another year. She didn't know who owned that shed, it was sort of in the middle of nowhere. She wondered when it would just fall over.

Just then something caught her eye. Something moved quite quickly and dashed into a gap in the old shed. At first it startled her and she jumped as if she were about to run. But then something stirred in her, a curiosity and overwhelming urge to go over to the shed.

She moved slowly and the dead grass crunched under her feet as she left the worn path and peered apprehensively at the shed. As she approached, she could just make out a small figure in the shadows. A small animal of some sort was just on the other side of the widely spaced boards. She was a little bit nervous but kept her course. Someone shouted and slammed a door in the distance and she jumped again.

"It's ok," she said moving ever so slowly toward whatever it was, "I won't hurt you." Then she heard a sound like a loud hum. It sounded like Grover from Sesame Street. She backed up not having ever heard that sound before. Surely she wasn't afraid of the Monster at the End of this Book but then again, she knew it wasn't Grover.

"Where are you?" she whispered. "What are you?" Two bright green eyes stared back at her as the daylight just touched the furry face through the slats in the shed. She made a little kissy noise and moved toward the opening where the door was hanging precariously off the hinge. She peered through the gap in the door and found herself staring into the eyes of a small gray and white cat. "Come on," she whispered, and the cat made that strange humming sound again. The cat moved forward toward Katie and the hum slowly became a very loud purr.

"Come on, that's it," she whispered smiling now, but the cat seemed too scared to come out. Katie moved the hanging door over just enough for her to sit on the stoop. She steadied the door, making sure it wouldn't fall and sat on the edge of the stoop. She felt something under her arm, and the cat climbed right into her lap. She stroked its neck, and the cat arched and pushed against her hand.

The fur was so soft, she'd never felt anything so soft before.

"Where did you come from?" The cat was now nuzzling Katie's neck and purring even louder. Katie giggled. "You sure are friendly." Katie put her arms around the cat to give her a little hug, but what she felt were some very boney ribs. She ran her hands along the cat. She was stroking the cat, but she was also assessing her condition. The cat had very bony shoulders and was very small, but her belly seemed a little bloated. Katie knew enough about animals to know that could be worms.

"Oh my, you are so skinny." The cat continued to purr, and hum, and walk back and forth, and up and down Katie. "I'm going to have to get you some food aren't I?" She looked down at the cat's face. The kitty's eyes were big and bright green and she had very long, bright white whiskers, and fantastic eyebrows that looked like antennae. Katie couldn't decide if she was white or gray. She was white on the bottom half and gray on the top as if she were wearing a gray blanket. The gray came down as if it was a mask on her face just cascading down over her eyes and stopping above her nose. Her nose and lips were a pale shade of pink perfectly nestled into her sweet, little white chin.

"You're not old enough to be out here on your own," Katie said quietly, "but obviously no one is taking care of you. You must be so scared and lonely out here." The cat circled twice on Kate's lap and then plopped down as if she had taken ownership of the little girl. Katie stroked the cat and sighed. She knew her parent's would never let her have a cat...not with her Mom's severe allergies. They couldn't even visit the home of someone with a cat. A fact that made life rather complicated socially. Katie reached carefully into her pocket and pulled out her phone. She awkwardly and one handedly swiped the screen and scrolled down through her contacts. Mom. She pressed the little yellow envelope she knew would send a text to her Mom at work, as she did everyday. With one hand under the her new friend's purring chin and one hand on the phone she painstakingly texted her Mom. "I'm home." She heard the familiar swoosh that she had sent the message.

"Right", she said placing her phone back in her pocket, "I don't have much time." She tilted her head down and craned her neck to see the face of the cat that was now fast asleep on her lap.

"Psst, kitty?" The cat made a noise between a purr and a snore. "You have to let me go if you're going to eat today. Kitty?" She moved slightly, and the cat readjusted herself. "Come on. I'm serious." She began to stand, and the cat reluctantly plopped off her lap and turned to look longingly at her as if to say *"Please don't leave me".*

"I'll be back. I promise," she whispered, leaning over and stroking the cat between the ears. The cat pressed up on Katie's hand while she purred. "Get back in there." She gently nudged the kitty who this time, resisted her hand. "You'll be safe. It's ok." She pulled the door back to where it had been narrowing the gap to the entrance hoping to deter anything that might consider entering. It was getting a bit colder and Katie pulled her hood up over her head as she stomped over the long grass and back onto the path. She turned back to see the little face of her new friend peering out of the shed. Her heart ached to leave her but knew she didn't have much time. A cold breeze blew her hood off her head. She smiled at the cat, motioned for her to hide and took off running toward the road. Katie's long red ponytail swung side to side as she ran. The little gray and white cat stood with her face just inside the gap and watched, motionless as Katie disappeared down the path and out of sight.

The Shed

The little white and gray cat, barely past kitten hood herself retreated back into the shed. She had found a small amount of rags and grass and made a little bed in the shadows. It was scratchy and she was cold but at least she had a roof over her head. Her tummy growled as she curled up in a ball. She squeezed her green eyes shut and her long whiskers twitched as she tried to force herself to sleep. She was very thirsty and tried not to worry about where to find water the next day. The snow was thawing and she had been able to find a few puddles and gutters that didn't seem too dirty. She was hungrier than usual and thought that little girl had been her ticket to a real home. She doubted she would come back. That scenario had played out more than once in her young life on the streets. She tried to forget all about the ginger haired girl. Why hope? It's not like anyone cares about a skinny homeless cat.

CHAPTER TWO

The Thompson's House

Katie arrived on her doorstep quite breathless. She had run the whole way knowing she only had the remains of an hour that was slipping away very quickly and her hungry and thirsty friend was waiting. She stood for a moment, hands on her knees and caught her breath.

"Ok," she said under her breath, "tuna and a bottle of water." No one would miss that. She reached inside her jacket, pulled out the lanyard and got her house keys. The key shook in her hand as she tried to steady herself and get it in the lock. She had to be quick. She turned and put her shoulder against the door expecting it to give. It didn't give. Locked. She had locked the door. She stood for a moment looking puzzled as she stared up at the door. That meant someone else had unlocked the door.

Her heart sank as she heard her mother's voice in the kitchen.

"Wait, I think that might be her," she heard her mother hang up the phone. "Katie? Is that you? Where have you been?" She was coming down the hallway quickly. She had a look of panic on her face but Katie knew what was coming. "Where have you been young lady?"

Katie couldn't speak. Her mind raced for an answer. Her mother put a firm hand on Katie's shoulder. "You texted me fifteen minutes ago and said you were home. Why would you lie to me? Do you know the thoughts that have been going through my mind? This is it young lady. I knew you were too young to stay home alone. I'll have to put you back in the after school program. I'm so disappointed in you Kate." Katie couldn't get a word in. "Where were you? I'm waiting." Her mother was not letting up.

"I...went for a walk," she said clumsily and unconvincingly. "What are you doing home?"

"What am I doing home?" Her mother sounded indignant. "That's none of your business. Went for a walk where?"

"I just went for a walk Mom. It was a nice day and I just decided to walk and enjoy the spring air now that winter is finally over." Her mother's heart softened. She knew exactly what she meant. Ohio winters were brutal.

"Why did you tell me you were home? How can I trust you again?"

Katie scrambled for an explanation. "I was almost home, I just hadn't come in. I had planned to come in. I was enjoying the spring air and decided to stay outside. You can see I wasn't gone long, it was only fifteen minutes ago." She pleaded with her mother. It was almost true.

"Well," her mother stood up straight looking a bit less threatening, "maybe I overreacted'" she paused, "we'll just let this one go this time...but you'd better not pull that stunt again. I was beside myself with worry."

"For fifteen minutes." Katie said, knowing as soon as she'd said it she had gone too far.

"Fifteen minutes is torture for a mother and you'd better watch yourself young lady before I change my mind."

"Sorry," Katie whispered sheepishly. She needed to stay on Mom's good side.

"I'm still undecided about you being here alone. I'll have to think about that. Now go put your books in your room. We're going to Uncle Mike's for dinner. That's why I am home early. It's Auntie Diane's birthday."

Katie heart sunk. How was she going to get back to her friend? What if they put her in that awful after school program again? This was a disaster.

The Shed

The little cat woke up from a dream. It was dark. She lifted her head slightly and looked in vain around the shed. She knew the truth, but she drew in a big breath through her nose hoping to smell some food deposited somewhere in the shed. Nothing. Just cold damp straw. Her heart dropped. She had really tried not to hope but she had been dreaming of food. Lots of food. She had often wondered what it was like in one of those big houses. She had peered in a few windows and seen cats and dogs sleeping on couches or cuddled up by the fire. Why was she all alone? She felt the familiar ache in her tummy and thought of the little girl with ginger hair. She must not have liked me, she thought. Maybe I smell. Maybe she thought I was just a skinny stray and I wouldn't fit in at her house. The cat lowered her head. Her green eyes slowly closed. She had survived the harsh winter scavenging in garbage cans and the odd mouse that came out when the deep freeze was gone. She had managed not to freeze to death but she was running out of hope and running out of will. It was a lonely life and maybe she should just go to sleep and not wake up.

CHAPTER THREE

Wethersfield, Ohio
Early Spring 2002

The little collie sat quietly at the edge of the road. His mouth was open and the end his tongue hung out just a little bit as he gently panted. He waited. His ears flicked mechanically like antennae with every noise. The sky was orange, red and yellow as the sun perched on the horizon. His ears pivoted as he heard an approaching sound. It came closer. The pup turned his head to see a vehicle creating a dust trail as it approached. His eyes brightened as he stood. His furry tail wagged back and forth faster and faster as the vehicle approached. He resisted the urge to run out into the road. He barked. A pick-up truck crested the hill and the little dog barked again, this time he jumped up onto his hind legs and batted at the air like an excited baby. The vehicle blew him off balance and into the ditch as it zoomed past him.

The collie puppy with the big brown eyes climbed out of the ditch and watched sadly as the vehicle continued down the road, around the bend and out of sight. The field was silent. He looked up at the sky just as the top of the sun slipped down below the horizon. The light gradually faded into darkness and the brown eyed collie puppy sat alone. He waited for someone to come and get him and take him home.

The Thompson House
Spring 2015

Katie's father pulled the Ford Explorer into the driveway at their house on Oakwood as she stared out the window. There was a bump at the end of the driveway that always jostled the family as they arrived home.

"Straight up to your room please Katie, it's a school night," said her father.

"Brush your teeth and straight to bed." He turned off the vehicle and the lights dimmed to black.

Katie stared out the window into the darkness. She longed to run from the car and straight to the shed. She remained composed, knowing she had to bide her time in order to execute her plan.

"Yes, Dad," she said obediently. She hopped down out of the vehicle and closed the door. She trotted up the front steps of the porch and waited while her Dad came and unlocked the door. He opened the door and motioned for her to go in. "Thanks Daddy," she said smiling up at him. He gave her a puzzled look. She had not called him Daddy in some time. He decided he liked hearing it and patted her on the head.

"You're welcome Katie Bug," he replied adoringly.

"Night!" Katie called as she sprinted up the stairs.

Katie's Mom came through the door carrying some leftover cake. "She go to bed already?" she asked her husband.

"Yep. "

Katie's Mom had not shared any of the details of Katie's mysterious whereabouts after school. She decided it was a minor infraction and Katie was a pretty good little girl. It was not necessary to involve her overprotective father. David had always said he wanted a son but when he became the father of two daughters something changed inside him. The whereabouts and well being of his three "girls" seemed to be the only thing that mattered in life.

The couple closed all the blinds, turned off the porch light and went side by side up the stairs.

"Jim says he thinks there's something living in the old shed," he said with a slight air of disgust. "Could be a coon Stace. Says, he's probably gonna have to shoot it."

"Dave! Why do you tell me things like that? asked Stacy. "I don't want to know." Katie's Mom peeled off at the top of the stairs and knocked on Katie's door. Katie had her ear pressed to the door and jumped back at the sudden knocking. "Do you have your pajamas on?"

"Uh, yeah," lied Katie.

Katie's mom opened the door and stared at her daughter as she stood in her clothes.

"What is the matter with you?" she asked with exasperation.

"I'm just about to change!" Katie said with much less respect than her mother was used to.

"I don't know what's going on with you but you'd better check your attitude. Go to bed. Good night," she said very sternly and walked out closing the door hard. "Great, she's not even a teenager yet," she muttered under her breath.

Katie lay in her bed staring at the ceiling. She heard the bathroom water run twice. She heard the toilet flush twice. She stared at the ceiling some more. The tick-tock of the clock seemed louder than usual. She waited and waited until she'd been lying there for over an hour and all had been silent. She looked over at the clock on her dresser. 11:09. *Gosh, were they asleep yet?* She quietly and ever so slowly folded the covers back. She very gently rolled out of bed and walked carefully and silently to the door. She opened it a tiny crack. The coast was clear. She had gone to bed wearing her robe. That could be explained if she was caught in the hallway so she decided against a coat. She quietly and carefully tip-toed down the stairs avoiding the creaky treads. She knew exactly where they were and everyone in the house knew what it sounded like when someone was on the stairs.

She tiptoed into the kitchen and quietly opened the pantry door. *Tuna. Perfect.* She thought. She turned to the utensil drawer and pulled out the can opener. *One last thing… The fridge, but that would be risky.* The light was so bright. Her parents were hopefully fast asleep but to open the fridge and fill the room with light just felt like such a risk of exposure. She remembered the cases of water by the back door and quickly slipped into the foyer. She grabbed a bottle of water and slipped all the items into her large robe pockets. She quietly put on her snow boots that were left in the foyer. In Ohio snow boots can't be put away until mid-May, at least. She suddenly remembered and grabbed two paper bowels from her mother's party supplies. She carefully opened the back door and stepped out into the night air. It was way too cold to be wearing a robe but she knew she had no choice. She slipped between the garage and the back fence knowing she could find her way to the shed in the dark. She couldn't risk being on the sidewalk.

The Shed

The little cat was sleeping very lightly. Every little scratch of a rodent or distant sound of a train kept her from being able to sleep. She was restless and felt very strange. It was a strange kind of tired that she had never felt before. Like something was draining her energy while she slept. Her mouth was dry but she knew going out to hunt for water this time of night meant possibly encountering something scary. She didn't have the energy for a scuffle.

She buried her face under her paws. She just wanted to disappear. She rolled over onto her side and stretched out. She let out a big sigh and just then she felt something moving in her tummy. Her tummy was so empty what could possibly be in there? Her drowsy eyes blinked slowly. Then she heard something. Something was outside the shed. Her heart pounded as she listened. What could it be? Those raccoons could be quite vicious. She didn't want to have to fight for her bed. She didn't have the strength to fight anything at all. She retreated as far back as she could and cowered in the shadows making herself as small and still as she could. It was coming closer. It was coming much closer and it was big, whatever it was.

Katie reached the shed. "I'm here," she whispered. Nothing. "Hello? It's just me," She whispered as she pulled back the door to make a little opening to look through. It was dark and she couldn't see anything. Dare she enter that pitch dark shed not knowing what could be in there? A chill came over her. The chill of fear. This was not okay. She should go back. There could be anything or anybody out here.

Suddenly she heard the hum, that Grover hum. A noise she had never heard a cat make before but she recognized it right away. She squeezed herself into the small opening and as her eyes adjusted to the darkness she could see the gray and white cat. The little cat looked as if she'd bounded out into the center of the shed and was standing with great enthusiasm as if to say "Here I am!" The room was filled with a great, long beautiful purr. Katie squatted down and the cat rubbed all along her legs almost knocking her down.

"Ok, ok," she giggled, trying to get herself down onto the shed floor without tripping over her robe or the cat. She sat cross legged and the little cat circled around her. She tried to get the tuna out of her pocket and felt the cat as she stretched all the way up her back as if she wanted a piggy back ride. The purr was deafening.

"Come around here," she said, reaching behind her. "The food is here." She struggled with the can opener and the overly affectionate cat who was purring so loud that now she wasn't so sure they wouldn't wake the neighbors. She scooped the tuna into the bowl getting most of it on the little cat's head which also happened to be in the bowl.

"There's nothing in there yet," she whispered, gently pushing the cat's head out of the way. The tuna hit the bowl and the little cat ate as if she had never seen food. She snorted as she wolfed down mouthful after mouthful. Katie was opening the water when the little cat stopped eating and looked up at her. Her green eyes were warm and gentle. The fur on her face was fluffy like a cloud. The cat looked at Katie lovingly and very slowly closed and opened her eyes twice while the sound of her purring filled the shed. Katie noticed a little twinkle in the cat's eye. She stood silently watching as the cat's eyes twinkled. Katie leaned over and poured the water in the bowl. The small kitty moved quickly to the water. She touched it once with her front right paw, plunged her head down and took a very long lapping drink of the water. Her tummy heaved in and out as she drank frantically. She looked up at Katie gratefully before returning to her long awaited meal.

"Twinkle," said Katie. That's what I'll call you.

CHAPTER FOUR

The Thompson House

Katie sat quietly at the dinner table looking unenthusiastically at her hamburger and poking it with her finger.

"Katie, you have not finished your dinner once this week," said her mother with concern.

"I ate most of it," she replied unconvincingly.

"You ate the bread," said her mother, her gaze narrowing, "and I hear you in the kitchen at night looking for leftovers so obviously you aren't getting enough food during the day. I'm trying to let you be a big girl but sometimes I have to step in."

Katie motioned for her mother to lean over and her mother obliged lowering her ear to Katie.

"I think it's these female changes that are making me feel funny and messing with my appetite," she lied. Her mother smiled knowingly.

"I see, "she said warmly." Go on then, you may be excused. But, Katie," she continued, "put it in the fridge so it will be there when you are hungry later." She winked at her daughter. Katie nodded, picked up her plate and carried it into the kitchen. She smiled as she put her plate in the fridge; she smiled at her father as she walked back through the dining room, her smile turning to a wide grin as she turned the corner for the stairs.

Well that couldn't have gone better, she thought. Leftovers for her friend? Check. Reason to be in the kitchen? Check. Perfect. Thank you puberty. Katie bounded up the stairs and into her room happily closing the door behind her.

Katie's parents sat at the dinner table quietly.

"She'll be a teenager soon and it is bound to get worse," Stacy said poking at her food.

"Jim said it's not a coon, " David blurted.

"I beg your pardon?" said Stacy thoroughly confused, "what's not a coon?"

"The critter in the shed," he said flatly, "Just a mangy old, stray cat. Probably should burn that old shed, it's a nuisance and it attracts strays."

"Mmm." Katie's mother was not really listening. She stood up and gathered up the plates. "I've got laundry," she said, but she was obviously distracted.

The next morning Katie sat quietly on the school bus clutching her backpack full of Twinkle's goodies. She had leftovers not only from her dinner the night before but also from her school lunch. This evening Twinkle would dine on hamburger, chicken nuggets and corn if she wanted it. That cat was eating like a queen and boy was she getting fat! Katie felt a great sense of accomplishment every time Twinkle's belly grew. The weather had been quite unpredictable over the past month between snow squalls and 70 degree days but she had managed to sneak a gallon jug of water out of the house so she didn't have to haul bottles of water to Twinkle. She had also successfully sneaked one of the fluffy afghans from her own bedding. It was between the comforter and the sheet so no one had noticed and Twinkle looked like royalty curled up in her new throne.

The bus came to a halt and Katie heard the familiar swoosh of the airbrakes. She happily bounded off the bus and trotted down the alley toward the old shed that housed her new best friend. Katie looked side to side to make sure the coast was clear, as she had been accustomed to doing and left the pathway toward the shed. She confidently pulled back the door and popped through the opening.

"Dinner time," she said happily but then, her face dropped. Twinkle was in her bed, lying on her side, panting furiously.

"What's wrong?" Katie asked, approaching slowly. She was afraid to touch her.

Twinkle was crying long low meows as if she were in great pain. What was she to do? How could she help? Katie popped back out of the shed into the daylight. There was no one around. There was no one to help. Was she dying? How could this be happening? Katie stood frozen with fear and desperation before crawling back through the opening. She would just have to take her home. Her parents would just have to deal with it. She would call her mom and tell her she had to come home. Twinkle needed a vet and she needed it right now!

Katie crawled across the shed floor and gently slid one hand under Twinkle trembling body. She started to lift and Twinkle cried out in great distress. Twinkle looked up at Katie, her eyes pleaded with Katie to not touch her. Just then Katie heard a strange new sound; it was a teeny, tiny sound. A sound so delicate she wasn't even sure she'd heard it. She pulled back the afghan near Twinkle's tail to reveal a tiny white kitten. She moved back up to Twinkle's head.

"Good girl," she said stroking her on the back of her neck, "you've done it, you have a baby kitten." Just then another tiny sound came from Twinkle's tail. Another kitten. Katie continued to stroke Twinkle's head and speak calmly to her. The love in her heart was so strong for her new friend and she felt as if she had a connection to someone, someone who needed her. Twinkle gave birth to two white kittens. They were very wet and very tiny. Twinkle's breath began to slow down. She was much calmer now.

"Just relax," Katie whispered. "Rest, you've done it."

She carefully scooped up the white kittens and brought them up to Twinkle's face. Twinkle began to nuzzle and lick them. She was exhausted but she was purring softly. Katie laid down next to her furry friend. "I love you

Twinkle," she said admiring Twinkle and her new family. Twinkle cleaned off all of her kittens and laid her head down. Just as she had finally relaxed her body suddenly tensed.

"What is it girl? What's wrong?"

Twinkle let out a loud painful cry. Katie looked up and down Twinkle's body to see if she could see anything. To her surprise another little face appeared between Twinkle's tail and the blanket. It was not crying, moving or making any noise at all.

"Oh no," Katie said gently plucking the tiny creature from within the blanket. Twinkle looked up at her with her warm, green worried eyes. Katie eyes were wide too as she stared down at the tiny creature. It was gray and it was much smaller than the others. Katie stroked its tiny head. Instinctively she began to rub the kitten and press gently on its belly. The kitten was so tiny she was afraid she would crush it. It was all gray but had a white star on its chest and 4 white paws like little white mittens. Twinkle meowed loudly as Katie tried to warm and revive the kitten. It wasn't working. She cupped it with her hands in an attempt to warm it up. The kitten was cold and not making any sound. Katie continued to try and warm the little kitten.

"I'm so sorry," she said finally. She moved toward Twinkle laying the kitten down next to her. Twinkle was not purring. Katie kept her hand on the kitten, dropped her head and began to sob. She let out a very long cry as she mourned for her friend's baby. She wiped her tears on her sleeve gathered herself and reached down to either comfort Twinkle or remove the kitten, she wasn't sure.

To her great surprise Twinkle was cleaning the little kitten, enthusiastically licking and nudging her kitten. She pulled it into her chest fur with her paws and licked determinedly. Unexpectedly the lifeless, little gray kitten with the white feet suddenly let out a very squeaky but very loud, long mew.

Katie's heart leapt in her chest! The kitten began to wriggle and lift its bobbly head searching for its mother. Twinkle licked and licked. Katie cried and laughed tears of joy.

"Oh good girl!" she exclaimed to her brave friend. "Good, brave Twinkle!" She wiped the tears from her eyes.

Katie stayed as long as she could but had to get home. She was amazed at how much Twinkle seemed to know about taking care of her kittens. Then she remembered something.

"I can't come tomorrow, I'm so sorry. Remember I have a dentist appointment? I didn't know this was going to happen today." Twinkle looked over her litter of kittens at Katie.

"You've got plenty of food and water and I'll see you Wednesday." The kittens were all cleaned and dried and nursing by the time Katie popped through the dilapidated shed door. She peaked back in to see Twinkle and her new family snug as a bug in a rug and her heart swelled with joy.

"I'll see you Wednesday." She blew Twinkle and the kids a kiss. "You'll be ok for one day without me." She said under her breath trying to convince herself and trying not to think about Mr. Kennedy.

The Shed

The sun was just starting to set and the new mother nuzzled and cleaned her new kittens. She had never known so much love. First the little girl with the long red hair and now three new little kittens to love. Perhaps being a stray cat was not all that bad. After all, she was fed and cared for. The little girl played with her and cuddled her and now this new joy. Life was definitely looking up. Twinkle gathered her two fluffy, white daughters and tiny gray son beneath her and curled her body around them. She was tired but it was a new kind of tired. A kind of tired she liked. Her heart was full as she lay her fluffy face down for a long sleep. Instinctively she wanted to stay awake with a newfound sense of protection but she felt the overwhelming urge to sleep. Her big green eyes were very heavy. The kittens all snored quietly and she drifted off to sleep.

Not knowing if it had been ten minutes or ten hours Twinkle was suddenly awaked by the sound of men's voices. Her eyes were very wide as she listened.

"You should burn it down." she heard someone say. Burn what down? They were very close to the side of the shed. She gathered her kittens tightly to herself and dared not even breathe.

"I don't know what I'm gonna do," shouted an unidentified man. "Maybe its gone." Twinkle jumped as someone pounded on the side of the shed, hard and several times. She gathered her kittens and retreated as far back as she could. The door was moving as if someone was prying on it with a tool of some sort. Twinkle's heart pounded in her chest. She was completely trapped. How would she protect them? What if

they were here to take the kittens? Suddenly light came through the opening. A bearded man wearing a black stocking hat poked his head through. He stared at Twinkle. Then his eyes focused on her kittens.

"Oh shhh..." His voice trailed off. "There's a litter of kittens in here!"

CHAPTER FIVE

Spring 2002

The little collie trotted along the country road. Having no choice, he'd spent the night alone at the edge of the field. He'd bedded himself down in some long grass and tried to keep warm. He hadn't slept much and he'd found nothing to eat. The morning sun was shining now and he felt slightly more optimistic. Surely the man in the stocking cap was coming back. Surely he hadn't left him out there all alone. If the old man wasn't able to come back for him then certainly he would send someone to pick him up and take him home. He hadn't done anything wrong that he could remember.

He half trotted for what felt like miles. He heard a sound. A car was coming. His scruffy, brown and black, floppy ears perked right up as if at attention. He sat down on the side of the road and waited. The sound was getting closer and closer. He waited patiently sitting at attention, his big brown eyes full of faith. He had faith that whoever was approaching was someone coming back for him. His tail wagged as the dust kicked up and a small white car made its way closer. The pup puffed out his chest and watched. The car came closer and closer and then, as his heart sank the white blur passed him right up. A cloud of dust covered the little dog's face. He watched as the car disappeared over the horizon. The sound subsided, the dust settled and the little collie dog let out a faint sigh. He stood up, thought good thoughts and continued trotting down the road with his bushy tail wagging effortlessly.

The day dragged on and the little dog stopped from time to time when he'd noticed some water pooling at the side of the road in a ditch. He would lap up whatever he could find in the puddles and have a less than refreshing drink throughout the day. He'd even discovered a hamburger wrapper. It didn't have anything in it but it sure smelled good and it was something in his tummy.

He had been trotting all day on that country road when he decided to see if there was anything to eat in the field. He hopped over the ditch at the side of the road and began sniffing and wandering back and forth across the field. He found the occasional bit of garbage but nothing very nice. The collie scavenged in the field not even sure what he was hoping to find. He heard several cars pass and barked to let them know he was there but he was too far away. He felt tiny in that big field. He hoped that he wasn't missing his ride home. The puppy looked up and noticed that the sun was starting to set again. He knew that he needed to look for shelter. He didn't want to spend another night in the open field. He looked at the openness of the field. The only thing that looked like shelter was the woods far off in the distance. He felt weak with thirst and hunger and looked again at how far off the woods were. He wondered what kind of animals might be in the woods. He didn't have much choice and began walking slowly, reserving his energy, toward the woods.

He'd made it about halfway to the woods when the little collie got a whiff of something, something sweet. He put his snout to the ground and began sniffing feverishly. Back and forth he sniffed and sniffed until his trusty little nose led him right to the apple in the middle of the field. The little dog nudged the piece of fruit with his nose. It was soft on the side that had been on the ground. He knew it wasn't ideally what he was looking for but he thought about how crunchy and sweet it would taste. He gently lifted the apple up with his mouth and lifted his head. He looked side to side. His stomach was calling all the shots. He couldn't resist the urge so he flopped down on his belly disappearing in the long grass and ate the apple, core and all.

Dr. Perry's Office
Spring 2015

"Looks pretty good Katie," said the dentist. "Keep up with that brushing and you'll keep those lovely choppers for a long time." Dr. Perry smiled at the young girl. Katie just wanted to get out of that dentist chair. She hadn't missed her daily visit with Twinkle since the day they met and she certainly wasn't comfortable missing today of all days. Twinkle's new little family was so tiny and vulnerable. Katie hopped out of the chair and hurried down the light blue hallway without saying goodbye or thank you. She emerged in the waiting room where her mother sat patiently reading a magazine.

"All set?" she asked.

"Yes, let's go!" Katie said impatiently. Katie's mother was getting quite fed up with her adolescent daughter's new attitude.

"Check your attitude Katherine." She said flatly. Katie ignored her mother's chastening. Her mind was racing as she tried to figure out how she was going to get to Twinkle tonight. Her older sister was coming home for Easter so she knew she would be expected to be home and spend a lot of time with her family. She loved her sister but she had much bigger things on her mind. Mr. Kennedy was going to shoot whatever was in the shed and she had to figure out how protect Twinkle, and now she had three kittens to worry about!

Her mother drove in silence as they turned down Oakwood Drive. Katie saw her sister Rachel's bright blue VW Golf in the driveway. She was always excited to see Rachel but Katie was terribly distracted. Maybe all the attention was going to be focused on Rachel, and she could sneak away for a few minutes, just to check and make sure all was well in the shed? Katie thought about that little gray kitten. He almost didn't make it. What if Twinkle was struggling to care for him? What if he went limp again?

Stacy stood holding the open car door. "You coming?"

Katie absent-mindedly climbed out of the vehicle.

The Thompson's House

Katie entered the front door first with her mother right behind her.

“Katie Bug!” Rachel exclaimed. Her arms wide open. Rachel was a tall pretty girl with very long brown hair and expressive, friendly eyes. She wore cool glasses and was one of those big sisters that just had it all together. Normally Katie Bug would have run across the room and jumped onto her sister in what they called a "spider hug". A spider hug was when little Katie would wrap her arms and legs around Rachel and squeeze as tightly as she could until Rachel nearly fell over. When Rachel left for Kent in the fall Katie had to be pried from her sister and her spider hug grip, while tears flowed down both their cheeks.

Now, Katie forced a smile and tried to look enthusiastic as she made her way across the room and gave her sister a less than "spider hug" worthy welcome. Rachel looked over at their mother. Katie's mom shrugged. Rachel crouched down to her little sister's level.

"I missed you," she said searching Katie's hazel eyes, "Why do you look sad?'

"I missed you too." Katie said quietly.

Just then their Dad came out of the kitchen. "No cavities Katie Bug?" Katie shook her head. "Good girl. Well, I have an announcement," he continued with enthusiasm. "Since we're all together for the long weekend I've booked us in at Ogelbay for our annual Easter treat!" He said triumphantly.

"No!" Katie cried.

Katie's mother, father and sister all looked her in shocked disgust.

"What do you mean no?" said her mother.

"I mean…we should be here… in our home, together." Katie softened her voice.

"Katherine, Oglebay is a family tradition. What is the matter with you? You used to love to go swimming and horseback riding with Rachel." Katie's mother was very unhappy with her daughter.

"We're going and that's that. Sit down at the dinner table and I don't want to hear another word about it. You should probably apologize to your sister. Maybe you should think about someone other than yourself young lady."

Katie's eyes lowered to the floor. She did feel sorry for how she reacted. Se did love Oglebay, but she *was* thinking about someone other than herself. She was thinking of FOUR others than herself.

"Sorry Rach." She put her arms around her sister's waist.

"It's ok Bug. We're going to have so much fun. You wait."

"When are we leaving?" asked Katie

"Tomorrow night. As soon as you get home from school," Dad said.

"Oh dear," thought Katie, *this is terrible.*" She choked back tears.

"Give me a hand David," said Katie's mom as she made her way to the kitchen. "Give the girls a moment while I get dinner."

Katie and Rachel sat at the dining room table. Rachel was asking Katie so many questions about school and what she'd been up to and just so many questions. Katie's thoughts were racing. Thoughts of running away from home; thoughts of Mr. Kennedy shooting poor Twinkle and her kittens.

Katie could just hear her mom and dad talking in the kitchen. Suddenly something caught her ear. She strained to listen over her sister's inane chattering. Katie could just barely hear her parents talking with very hushed voices.

"Jim said it's a stray," said David.

"What's a stray?" asked her mother.

"The critter in the shed," he replied.

"Oh that."

"THAT is a stray and now she's apparently had a litter of kittens. We'll be overrun by strays, Stace." Katie's father was not a fan of stray cats.

"What's he gonna do?" asked Katie's Mom.

"What he should do is drown them in a bucket," he replied loudly.

In the dining room Katie's mouth dropped and her eyes widened as she stared in shocked silence at her sister while she chattered on obliviously.

Katie's mom dropped the knife she was using to cut the tomato. She shot her husband a look of horror. He winked and shook his head. Katie's Mom's look of horror softened to a good natured smile and she stuck her tongue out at him. She knew Jim Kennedy would never do that and her husband would never actually suggest that. Jim might shoot a groundhog or a raccoon but he would never kill innocent strays, let alone tiny kittens. She carried the salad bowl over to the counter near her husband. She leaned over and gave him a tender kiss on the cheek.

"You're an old softy," she said. "You're not fooling anyone." Katie's Dad puffed out his chest and made his best manly mean face.

"Yeah right," said Kate's mom as she left him and his puffed up chest in the kitchen.

Katie could barely manage a forkful of food that night. She felt as if she might be sick.

"You're not eating much Bug," said Rachel. Katie just stared at her plate. Rachel looked over at their mother. Her mother mouthed the word "hormones". Rachel nodded and smiled knowingly.

The Shed

Twinkle finished sharpening her claws on the inside boards of the old shed. She'd better be ready for the fight of her life. The men had left her and her kittens for now but she had a distinct feeling they would be back. She stretched her whole body out along the shed floor and shook herself. As much as she stretched and sharpened, she was still young and very small. She worried what might be coming in the night. She worried what could happen in the morning. She didn't know if she'd be able of take care of herself and her family. The girl with the red hair had not come at all that day. That had never happened before.

Twinkle looked at her kittens. They were all curled up in a little pile of fluff, whiskers, pink noses and tender little paw pads. Her heart swelled with love for them. She padded over to the small opening in the shed door and gazed out through the hole. Her little pink nose was just illuminated by the last light of the day and her green eyes sparkled. The sun was setting over the long grass and there was no sign of the ginger haired girl. Twinkle let out a long sigh as the sun disappeared and the darkness set in.

Darkness fell over her white and gray face. She stared out at the darkness and suddenly, instinctively she knew what she must do. The instinct was very strong. It was as if a lion had begun to grow in her heart. It was so obvious. Her whiskers twitched and her shoulder muscles flexed. It was as if she could not control the urge. She would have to gather up her family and get out of there before those shouting men came back. She did not know where she could go. She wished the little girl would appear but she wasn't coming and Twinkle knew she didn't have much time.

CHAPTER SIX

The Thompson's House

Rachel Thompson was fast asleep, glad to at last be in her own room and in her own bed. She had grown up in that house in Struthers, Ohio. She knew that neighborhood like the back of her hand. She was so thankful to be home. She wished she knew what was wrong with her normally cheerful, playful, little sister but for now there was something comforting about being home. When she had crawled into her own bed she knew it was going to be a deep sleep she had not experienced since moving into the noisy dorm.

Rachel had been sound asleep for some time when she thought she heard a knock at her door. She opened one eye. There it was again. It took her a moment to get her bearings as she wasn't entirely sure where she was but then she remembered. She sat up in bed and pulled the lamp string. The room was filled with warm light and she squinted.

"Come in," she said quietly, recognizing that it was the middle of the night. The door creaked as it opened and there was little Katie Bug, her eyes swollen and red. Katie stood in the doorway in her pajamas.

"What is it?" Rachel asked tenderly. Katie was absolutely Rachel's favorite person in the whole world. She would never forget when she had learned that Katie was coming and then the day they had brought Katie home from the hospital. She thought her heart would pop with love. Rachel thought of Katie as *her baby*. She knew officially their mother was the mother but Rachel nurtured her little sister as if she were her own.

"Come here, Katie Bug." Rachel held her arms open. Katie flung herself into her sister's arms and let out a long cry. Rachel's shoulder was immediately drenched in her sister's tears. "What is it?" Rachel pleaded.

Katie looked up at her big sister, tears streamed down her face. “You have to promise not to tell,” Katie cried.

“Yes, yes, what is it?” Rachel pleaded again.

“PROMISE!” Katie cried.

“Ok, I promise!” Rachel tried to keep her voice down.

“I have a secret,” Katie continued, “Mom and Dad don’t know and you CAN’T tell them.”

“I won’t, I promise.” Rachel confirmed her former promise.

“You know the old shed in the lot behind Kennedy’s house?”

“Yes,” said Rachel.

“I have a friend in there. She’s my best friend and she doesn’t have a home,” Katie continued. Rachel’s heart pounded in her chest. Did Katie have a homeless friend?

“Ok…” she said, trying to comprehend.

“Mr. Kennedy’s going to shoot them or drown them,” Katie was sobbing. Rachel was now very confused and very concerned.

"Shoot or drown who?" she asked.

"Twinkle and her kittens!" Katie continued blubbering. Rachel felt a sigh of relief.

"Oh, I see," she was greatly relieved that Katie did not have a homeless school friend that Mr. Kennedy was going to shoot or drown.

"I have to rescue them," Katie pleaded with her sister and Rachel could see just how broken hearted her little sister was. "Dad's making us leave all this weekend and Mr. Kennedy's gonna…" She couldn't finish the sentence.

"Shhhhh, it's ok…"

"It's NOT ok! "She's my best friend. I was there with her when her kittens were born yesterday. You should have seen how brave she was. You should see them! It was only yesterday Rachel! They are just tiny. She won't be able to protect them." Katie was obviously beside herself over these strays. Rachel knew that day old kittens were pretty fragile. She had always loved animals. She certainly loved Katie and she decided to help her.

"There's a no kill shelter just in town. Let's get Mom and Dad and we'll all take them to the shelter." Rachel thought it sounded reasonable.

"NO!" cried Katie. "It was Dad who said they should be drowned! He can't know! Mom can't know! She didn't even say anything! They both think they should be drowned in a bucket! I heard them talking! You promised!"

"Ok, ok," said Rachel calmly narrowing her eyebrows. *Would her parents do that? Why would Katie make that up?*

"We have to get them tomorrow, we'll be gone after that," said Katie, trying to sound less hysterical.

"Don't you have school tomorrow?" Rachel asked carefully.

"Yes I do…" Katie's face scrunched up as she began to break apart again. Rachel's heart broke for her little sister.

"Well," she said coyly, "you'll just have to skip school," Rachel continued matter-of-factly. Katie's eyes widened in surprise.

"Really?" she said with slight hope in her voice.

"Yeah…I'll help you," Rachel said knowing that skipping school was hardly a capital crime. Katie threw her arms around her sister and kissed her all over her face.

Rachel dried Katie's tears and the two sisters planned out "*Operation Twinkle Rescue*" to be carried out the next day. Rachel would offer to take Katie to school in her car. They would divert behind the grocery store, get a box, rescue Twinkle and her kittens from the shed before mean old Mr. Kennedy could get his gun, or his bucket, and take them to the safety of the local shelter. If Katie couldn't have Twinkle for herself at least she would know she and her kittens were safe.

The Shed

Twinkle looked out into the chilly night air. The ginger haired girl was not coming. She summoned up all her courage. She knew the loud men could come back at any moment. She wasn't sure what was out there in the cold dark night but it had to be better than the fate that awaited them tomorrow.

She nuzzled and licked her fluffy gray son. She felt around his sleeping neck with her mouth instinctively finding the right spot. He woke up and cried a little mew. She gently put just enough pressure with her teeth on his neck skin to lift him but not injure him. He went limp and tucked his tail up. Twinkle looked at her daughters. Where would she go? Where would she put him all alone while she came back for the others? Who would protect the girls while she was gone? She wasn't at all sure about this but knew it must be done. The instinct was overwhelming.

She turned back to the opening, kitten hanging from her mouth and slipped out into the chilly night air.

CHAPTER SEVEN

The Thompson's House

The Thompson family breakfast table was quite lively the next morning. Whatever cloud had been hanging over little Katie seemed to have gone. That's the way it is with hormones.

"So you're taking Katie to school Rachel?" Stacy Thompson asked her eldest daughter.

"Yep," Rachel's reply was muffled by her mouthful of eggs. "I'll bring her home too," she continued after she had swallowed. Maya and I are going to the mall and we'll swing by and pick her up on our way back."

"That's convenient Katie. You won't have to ride the bus." Katie nodded to her mother taking a big bite of toast. "I see you've got your appetite back sweetheart, I'm happy to see you eating." Katie nodded again taking a big swig of her orange juice. She flashed her mother a smile. Katie and Rachel's father appeared at the table. He was in his pajamas.

"Aren't you going to work today Dad?" Rachel asked, trying to sound casual.

"Nope," he replied as he scooted his chair in. "Mom's not either…" his sentence drifted off as if he'd just thought of something. "In fact, Katie Bug's the only one with school today, maybe we just let her skip and we can set off to Oglebay after breakf…"

"No!" Katie interrupted him. "I, uhh have an algebra test today," she said awkwardly. Rachel just kept eating as if she wasn't paying attention but her heart was pounding.

"An algebra test the day before Easter break? That doesn't sound very nice," said their mother.

"Tell me about it." Katie said forcing her voice to sound calm.

"Ok, then we'll leave when you get home from school. Gosh, that just sounds wrong….algebra test indeed," Katie's mother said clearing empty plates.

Katie shot Rachel a wide-eyed stare. Rachel returned her stare with a knowing "*It will all be fine. Be cool,*" look.

Mr. Kennedy's Garage

David Thompson and Jim Kennedy had been friends and neighbors for many years. The two men were chatting in the open doorway of Jim's immaculate garage. Jim turned and began searching for something while they talked. He looked high and low. He opened and closed cabinets. He even looked in the garbage can.

"Whatcha huntin' for?" asked David, sipping his coffee. The two men often would visit one another on weekends and holidays but never went much further than their respective garages.

"A box, any kind of cardboard box," Jim replied. "Sarah recycles everything and I do mean everything and the recycling just went out. I can't find a box to save my life." Jim finally reached under his workbench and pulled out a 5 gallon bucket.

“What’s that for?” asked David.

“The strays in the shed,” Jim replied. “Sarah wants me to take care of them.”

David stared at the bucket remembering his joke to Stacy. “You wouldn’t,” David said cautiously. Jim narrowed his brow. He looked at the bucket.

“Oh…Oh…NO! David, how long have you known me? I couldn’t do that. Poor choice of words," he chuckled. "By take care of them I mean she wants me to go get them and take them up to the shelter. At least we would know they would have food and shelter and Linda doesn’t adopt those animals out to anyone but good families.”

"How's she doing these days?" asked David sympathetically.

"Don't know really," replied Jim. "It's so sad. How long's it been since Kevin died? Four years?" Jim asked still searching the garage. David nodded. "It can't be, really?" Jim stopped and stared at his friend.

"Yeah, she's been running that shelter at least that long. It's all she does," David replied.

"Well, I'm sure it gives her a sense of purpose and she couldn't be lonely with all those animals." He looked at the bucket. "This will have to do. I'll just have to find something to put over the top." Jim looked around the shelves in the garage.

"Oh they're not going to like that," said David.

"Dude, I don't HAVE A BOX." Jim laughed.

"I know, I'm just sayin," laughed David "I better come with you. I'm gonna love watching you try to put stray cats in a bucket."

"Yeah I bet you will. Hey, grab that gas can too. There's an old Weedwacker up there and I'm gonna see if I can knock those weeds back a bit on the fence before they get too overgrown." Jim motioned to a large gasoline can on the shelf.

"Got it," said David and the two men set off for the old shed.

Struthers, Ohio

Katie and Rachel had already been around to the back of the grocery store and found a lovely big box. Katie had sneaked a blanket into her backpack in lieu of the books she certainly wouldn't need at school that day. Rachel parked her car behind the old laundromat where no one would see it and the two girls crept carefully through the backyards carrying the padded cardboard box. They had to be very careful. It would have been a cinch had their mom and dad been at work but still they had to execute their plan to rescue Twinkle. The two girls reached the opening to the clearing that housed the old shed. They checked to make sure the coast was clear. They crouched down low feeling very exposed by the open lot. Just as they reached the shed Rachel jerked

Katie's arm and pulled her round the side of the shed.

"Get down," said Rachel, pushing her sister's shoulder. Someone was coming.

The voices were in the distance but they were getting closer. Coming up the worn path and headed directly to the old shed were their Dad and Mr. Kennedy. Mr. Kennedy was carrying a five gallon bucket and in their father's right hand was a large can of gasoline.

CHAPTER EIGHT

Wethersfield, Ohio
Spring 2002

The little collie had curled up in some long grass and tried to soak up any of the limited sunshine of the day. He dreamed of food and a warm bed. His little nose twitched as the chilly breeze wafted through the field. He curled himself tighter and tighter in an effort to stay warm.

His dream was interrupted by a strange sound. He lifted his head. Something was coming. He drew in a long inhale through his nostrils. Something or someone was definitely coming his way. He slowly and carefully rose up to a sitting position. Across in the distance he could just make out a bright orange figure. A person! Maybe it was the man in the stocking cap come back to take him home! He jumped to his feet intent to run to the man. Instead, when he got up and his head was above the long grass he found that he was face to face with a big fat turkey. It gobbled at him and waddled past him as if something was chasing him. The collie was confused. What was chasing the turkey? He watched the turkey run by and looked back at the figure in bright orange. The collie leapt forward and started to run to the man.

All of a sudden BAM! The noise was louder than anything the little dog had ever heard. His weary legs turned to the woods and he began to run before his brain could even catch up. His breath heaved as he charged faster and faster toward to the woods. His mouth was dry with thirst as he bounded over the long grass.

The sound of the shot echoed through the valley and the little dog ran and ran. He reached the edge of the woods and despite his fear of what might be in there he sprinted through the briars at the edge of the woods. He jumped over log after log. He couldn't stop running if he wanted to. The brush was getting thick as he got deeper and deeper into the forest. His paws bled as he caught them on the bramble and brush. His tongue hung from his mouth, dry with thirst.

Finally, when his body could take no more, the little collie stopped running. He looked around his surroundings. The forest was eerily quiet and he was deep into it. Something moved near his front paws. A little mouse darted out of the leaves and shot along a fallen tree on the ground and leapt into the underbrush.

The little collie let out a sigh. He would have to find his way out of the forest before nightfall and he desperately needed to find water. He forced his tired legs to start walking. He kept his nose to the ground looking for any morsel of food. He wasn't sure if he was even headed in the right direction. It seems all hope was lost.

Mission Street Rescue
Spring 2015

It was a sunny Thursday morning and it was opening time at the Mission Street Rescue. Linda Morrison exited her Chevy Cruz and made her way, arms loaded to the front entrance of the building. She placed the key in the lock of the big glass door of the cinder block building as she did every morning.

"Good morning Liebchen and Gretchen. Good morning Luke," she said cheerfully as her neighbor, Luke rounded the corner walking his two German Shepherds.

"Busy day today?" he asked as the two big dogs approached Linda for a head scratch.

"Well, I never know really. I'm almost full so hopefully lots of successful adoptions today." Linda adjusted the dog food in her arms and gave the dogs a stroke.

"Let me help you, " Luke said reaching for the door. Linda had purchased the old grocery store on Mission Street four years earlier with the life insurance she'd received when she was unexpectedly widowed at the age of 36. She'd quit her job as a medical secretary and over the last 4 years Linda and the Mission Street Rescue volunteers had successfully homed hundreds of stray pets and it made her life seem much more meaningful.

It was a humble life. Linda barely made enough money to get by and always put herself second to her furry little treasures. She had never been very high maintenance but now, even more so as a widow, it was ponytails and t-shirts, she didn't have any need for any more than that.

Her arms were loaded with various bags of dog and cat food she'd gathered the evening before from generous town people who faithfully supported her mission and Linda waited as Luke pushed open the door. The long string of bells she had hung above the door jingled as she entered. The two big German Shepherds attempted to enter.

"No girls, we're going for walkies." Luke gently tugged on their leashes.

"You have a great day... and thank you," Linda called out as she entered the front of the shelter and closed the door behind her. Luke guided his dogs back to their morning walk and gave her a friendly wave.

"Good morning family," she said cheerfully as a small wave of movement came over the room and all the sleeping animals. Pete the parakeet squawked and the whole room slowly came to life.

The puppy's white velvety eye lids flickered as he heard the door open. The young dog opened his eyes sleepily and lifted his head. It was her. It was the woman who had been so kind to him after his horrible ordeal. The small, mostly white pit bull with pink lips, floppy pink ears and blue eyes kept his chin on the floor. He watched as Linda did her morning routine. She made various trips in and out of the door and each time the bells jingled the puppy's heart leapt with hope. He was so fond of her after she had rescued him that awful day. He tried not to think about it but he was so grateful. He was scared at first of course, but over the last two days his fear had transformed to absolute adoration. He watched as Linda carried in bags of food, piles of newspaper and several gallons of bleach. She flipped a switch and rows of low florescent lights flickered on. Linda stood in the middle of the big room.

"Right, who is first?" she said looking at the many cages of dogs who desperately needed a walk.

The puppy closed his eyes and pretended to be asleep. The woman with the long ponytail and a t-shirt that simply said "Adopt" approached the cage containing the large yellow Labrador on the end row. She spoke cheerfully to the old girl as she opened the door and clipped a long leash on the large, fluffy dog. They walked right in front of the puppy's cage and out the door they went. The puppy slowly lifted his head off the little pillow at the end of his cage. He stood up and walked to the front. He looked down the row of cages. He walked back to the pillow, circled a couple of times sluggishly, and plopped down letting out an involuntary sigh. He didn't understand where he was. He was very confused. He had always been a good boy and he didn't know why the man was so angry. He was kind and gentle and wanted nothing but to have someone to love. His little heart sunk wondering what would happen to him but at least for now he was safe and away from that horrible man.

The Shed

Rachel Thompson had never been so angry in all her life. She squeezed Katie's hand to keep her in place behind her and against the side of the shed.

What were they going to do? Was she going to jump out and confront her father and Mr. Kennedy before they got anywhere near Twinkle and the kittens? she thought.

"Shhh, "she whispered to her little sister. "Don't move a muscle."

The two men were getting closer, and Rachel strained to hear their conversation. They could hear muffled voices, and then suddenly it went quiet. Rachel was just about to jump out from the side of the shed when she heard her dad's voice.

"Oh great, they're gone," he said sounding very disappointed. Rachel looked back at Katie and narrowed her eyebrows. Katie shrugged feeling both a sense of relief and panic.

"Aw man, she must have moved the litter in the night," Jim said, "We'll have to go look for them."

Katie's chest swelled with pride. *Good Twinkle,* she thought. But her thoughts were scattered. *They were going to go look for them? Why? Were they really going to hunt Twinkle down just to rid the street of her and her stray kittens? How were they going to find Twinkle before her Dad and Jim Kennedy who were bound and determined to kill her?*

The two crouching girls were stock still and holding their breath as they waited for the coast the clear. They could hear the voices trailing off as they two men made their way back down the path. Rachel peered around the side of the shed and could see the figures of the two men, five gallon bucket in hand as they determinedly marched toward the center of town.

"Now what?" Katie asked trying not to cry.

"It's ok," Rachel said calmly pulling Katie into herself. "Cats do this when they sense danger. Twinkle did the right thing. We just have to find her before Dad."

Rachel wiped her sister's hair from her face. "It's not going to be easy. Ugh why today of all days does he have the day off?" Rachel gathered herself.

"She's probably found somewhere to hide. Think of all the places you can that a cat would be able to hide." Rachel knew they didn't have much time to find this needle in a haystack. There were a million places for a cat to hide in the neighborhood.

"She's probably so scared," Katie said quietly still trying not to cry. Twinkle was not old enough to be out on her own and how would she take care of her kittens without Katie's help?

"I know," Rachel comforted her sister. "But we will find her. Just don't panic. We have to stay calm. Twinkle needs us to stay calm and think." Rachel paused. "Katie, try to think. Where would she go?" Katie's eyes moved back and forth around the open lot. There were some woods to the east. *Would she go to the woods?* There wasn't really any shelter in the woods. Katie had found Twinkle in the shed. She would be looking for some sort of structure to keep her kittens hidden. They were looking for a structure.

CHAPTER NINE

Mr. Kennedy's backyard

Jim Kennedy and Dave Thompson sat at the picnic table behind the Kennedy's house. The Kennedy's owned the biggest property in town. The home had more of a farm feeling than any other lots on the block. The lawns were always mowed and Mr. Kennedy was a gardening man. His prized tomatoes were the hit of the harvest season. Sarah Kennedy emerged from the screen door carrying a tray with some sandwiches and placed it on the table as she slipped her legs over the bench seat and joined the men.

"No luck then?' asked Sarah as she doled out the sandwiches onto white plastic plates.

"Nope," Jim said, "they're gone Sarah. They're just gone."

"You must find them," Sarah said boldly. "We know the mother is young, those kittens are brand new and something could eat them."

Jim knew better than to argue with his wife when it came to animals.

"We'll look again after lunch but Dave's headed to West Virginia this afternoon so if we don't find them I don't know what else we can do." Jim said taking a bite of his turkey sandwich.

"Well you'll have to find them quickly," she replied as a slight breeze blew back her pretty blonde hair. Sarah Kennedy was a curvy and very attractive woman. Jim was powerless when he looked at her. Dave shot Jim a look, smirked and shoved his turkey sandwich deep into his mouth.

"Yes dear," Jim said sheepishly.

An old abandoned desk

Twinkle curled tightly around her nursing kittens. It was dark but not dark enough. She had not found a very adequate place to hide in the night, but it was her only option in her hurry to move her family. The sun had risen during her search for shelter and was now beaming into the opening of the desk. Twinkle could hear voices and she retreated as far back as she could go into the shadows. The young mother was trapped and she was very thirsty. The kittens seemed to be draining all her energy and her dry tongue stuck to the roof of her mouth. Twinkle knew that she was trapped there until nightfall. She could never leave her kittens with all that light beaming in and the voices nearby. She also knew that she would be seen in the bright light of day. She didn't even know where she could find water. She looked lovingly at her three brand new kittens. They were so tiny and hadn't opened their eyes. She thought back to the shed and the ginger haired girl. She closed her eyes and dreamed of tuna, long drinks of milk and her green eyed friend.

The girls were running out of hope and running out of time. Lurking around the side lots and alleys was not proving to be fruitful at all. Having to stay hidden had greatly complicated an already complicated situation.

"Katie, I hate to say this but we had better go move my car. Dad and Mr. Kennedy will make their way over there eventually and I'll have a hard time explaining that," Rachel said.

"I don't care what they think and we don't have to explain anything," Katie said flatly.

"I know what you mean, but seriously we can't help Twinkle if we're in trouble," Rachel reasoned with her little sister.

"Ok, ok."

The girls carefully made their way through the back lots on Second Street. They hesitated between two houses and looked at the road. There was going to have a be a quick dash across the road in order to reach the laundromat. They looked left and right and saw the coast was clear. They held hands as they quickly dashed across the road. Just then the two men emerged around the corner of Second and Maple. The two girls saw the figures approaching and ducked into the alley just short of their target. Crouching, they held their breath as the voices got closer.

"Please don't see my car," whispered Rachel. "Just keep walking straight, just keep walking straight," she chanted quietly as if she could control the men.

"Rache..."

"Shhhh," replied Rachel.

"No, Rachel. Look!" Katie eyes were fixed upon an old desk that was shoved against an old chain link fence behind the Laundromat. It was covered by the hanging branches of the old willow tree but she could see the bottom half of the desk. The desk was old and dry-rotted from being left out in the elements. Rachel and Katie looked at the desk, looked at each other and back to the desk. The bottom left drawer was missing.

The abandoned desk

Twinkle heard men's voices and stood up protectively in front of her kittens. Soon she heard another voice, a familiar voice. Was that the ginger haired girl? But then, another voice. Too many people. Too much danger. The little cat's heart raced with anticipation. She looked at her helpless kittens. They were trapped. She knew she could not carry them all, and she knew they could not all make a run for it. The kittens couldn't even see yet, let alone run. Obviously, the men had returned and it was time for desperate measures. The gray and white cat peeked around the corner of the desk very carefully. She saw the ginger haired girl and her heart swelled. But the girl was not alone. She heard the men's voices again.

That familiar feeling swelled in her chest. She took a deep breath. Her instinct was engaging and she didn't like what it was saying, but she knew she didn't have time to think. She had to move very quickly and there was no time for long goodbyes. She crawled slowly back to her three little kittens all sound asleep in a perfectly circular pile. She stared at them and blinked slowly. She inhaled deeply through her nose and tried to savor their smell. She slowly nudged each one who responded with the tiniest little purr. Twinkle licked them each on their wet soft heads. She took a deep breath as her eyebrow whiskers brushed against the top of the desk. She nuzzled and savored each one. She took another big breath, turned her body carefully away from the kittens, and she slinked into place just behind the opening so that she was concealed from view.

The two girls carefully but swiftly approached the desk. Katie crouched down and got on all fours. The crumbled asphalt poked at her uncomfortably through her jeans and created imprints on the palms of her hands.

"Twinkle?" she whispered. Just then she heard the familiar indescribable sound that Twinkle made. She lowered her neck as far as she could, crouching to the lowest level she could get to. She was face to face with Twinkle.

"I found you!" She whispered loudly, unable to control her joy.

Twinkle's eyes softened for a moment and her big green eyes closed for a long pause. When she opened them she gave Katie a little hum and a purr. Twinkle pushed her head up against the bottom of Katie's hand. Purring loudly, she pressed her head again on Katie's hand. Katie giggled at her affection. Suddenly Twinkle made a mad dash. She shot straight under Katie's arm and was out in the alley before Katie could grab her.

"NO!" Katie shouted.

"Shhhhh," said Rachel, "They're coming!"

Katie saw Twinkle run like a gray shot down the alley. She reached the end of the alley and turned left in front of her father and Mr. Kennedy.

"There she is!" shouted Mr. Kennedy and the two men gave chase.

"Get the kittens, quick," said Rachel.

Katie didn't have time to think, and she reached blindly into the darkness at the back of the desk. The two men would be back soon, and she had to get these kittens. Somehow she knew with an amazing level of certainty that Twinkle had given her very clear instructions only moments ago. Katie felt the warmth of the sleeping kittens and carefully but quickly pulled them out and placed them in the box Rachel was holding out. Katie looked down the alley and her heart ached for Twinkle. If she chased after them then all kittens would be in danger. She was torn.

What about Twinkle? If Twinkle had not created that diversion their Dad would have seen the girls or at least seen Rachel's car, and they would have been caught! Twinkle was a hero. Twinkle was the ultimate momma even if she was young. But, what if they caught her? Katie's heart was breaking thinking of her little friend running for her life. As if reading her sister's mind Rachel reassured the little girl.

"They'll never catch her Katie Bug. She'll be fine." Katie looked up at her sister's warm eyes and fought back the tears. "Be brave, like Twinkle. She did the right thing. Let's get the kittens safe." Katie nodded and dropped her head.

Rachel lifted her chin. "Really Bug, she'll be fine! We have to do what she wanted us to do. She's trusting in you."

Katie felt a swell of duty in her heart. The closest thing to motherhood she had ever known. She quickly peeked into the box. The kittens made tiny little mews as they wobbled unsteadily, trying to find each other. The two sisters ran carefully, carrying the box of kittens down the alley and disappeared behind the Laundromat.

CHAPTER TEN

Mission Street Rescue

Linda Morrison had finally finished taking all the dogs for their morning walk and done the feeding. The puppy on the end was asleep when she came in so she didn't wake him. He'd been through quite an ordeal and he appeared to be sleeping so peacefully.

Linda's went about her usual routine of walking all the dogs who seemed interested in going outside first and then filling the food and water bowls and take care of anyone who still needed to go out. It had already been a long morning but taking care of these creatures was most assuredly, a labor of love. Linda stood at the sink and brushed the hair from her face. She turned the tap off and lifted the bowl from the sink. One more bowl of food and water for the dogs was needed, and she could turn her attention to the cats who were all still pretty much asleep.

She turned from the stainless steel counter and carried the last water bowl down the row of steel cages to the last pen in the row. She pulled back the latch quietly and looked at the sleeping pit bull puppy with the pink lips. He was her newest arrival and she knew he was frightened. She didn't want to startle him but she wanted him to wake up before she came into the pen. Of course Linda knew that pit bulls had a bad reputation. She also knew that all dogs who had been abused were likely to defend themselves and pit bulls were no more likely than any other breed to act out in fear.

Linda jiggled the latch slightly to make a little noise and saw the puppy's nose twitch. He slowly opened his eyelids to reveal sparkling blue eyes. He looked as if he were pink and covered in white velvet. His pale blue eyes were surrounded by soft pink flesh. The only other color on him was a little speckling of brown on his nose. His pink paw pads were just visible as he lay his head between his front paws. His skin fell in folds of white velvet wrinkles on his forehead as he lifted his non existent eyebrows. Linda heard the muffled but distinct thud of the puppy's tail as it hit the pillow, first slowly and then with increasing speed and intensity. He kept his head on the pillow as if he wasn't sure what Linda was going to do. She couldn't help but allow herself to grin. He was quite a big dog but she could tell he was very young. He had a wide chest and wide set blue eyes. He was big now, but one day he was going to be enormous.

"Good morning Lucky," she whispered, so as to not alarm him. The pup kept his head down on the pillow but his hopeful eyes were locked on Linda. His floppy ears perked up as he watched carefully while Linda placed the bowl of water in the corner. She picked up the empty food bowl and stepped just outside to a bag of food leaning on the steel pens. She scooped up some food with a plastic coffee can. The puppy heard the food and quickly lifted his head revealing a long, fresh, seeping wound that circled his entire neck. Linda kept one eye on him as she filled the bowl, smiling and speaking softly. She turned to step back in with the pup and Lucky immediately dropped his chin back down to the pillow.

"It's ok," she said. The pup stared at Linda with wide, hopeful, bright blue eyes. His tail continued to thud. "Come on," she whispered. His little pink nose and lips twitched as he sniffed the smell of the food wafting on the air. "You're ok now." Linda crouched down and pushed the food around the bowl with her finger.

The pup began to inch forward. His belly slid slowly onto the floor inches at a time. "That's it," she encouraged him. Linda continued to coax the pup over the food bowl and he slithered over, tail wagging, eyes smiling as he slid slowly toward her on his belly.

Linda began to stand up. The puppy froze. Linda froze. "It's ok..." she began but it was too late. He was back in the corner on the pillow, chin on the floor. Linda's heart broke for him. She was going to have to tend to that chain wound. She slid down the side of the cage and sat on the floor and started the process again.

It was mid morning by the time Linda finished filling all the upturned cats' water and changing newspaper. She was short of volunteers because of the Easter holiday and she knew she would have a long weekend ahead of her. Her animal family didn't know it was Easter weekend and neither did their bladders or bellies. No rest for Linda.

The chimes on the door jingled snapping Linda to attention from behind a pile of newspapers.

"Morning," she called out to a small family who had entered the shelter. "How can we help you?" she enquired.

"We're looking for a puppy," said a tall teenaged girl with big brown eyes and long beautiful hair. She was perfectly built. The kind of female who had always made Linda feel soft-boned, frumpy and almost as if she were a different species. The young lady looked like an Abercrombie & Fitch model. Her skin was perfectly unblemished and she had not one split end on her whole head. Linda wondered if she even owned a blow dryer.

"Any certain kind in mind?" she asked.

"We're not married to any certain breed," said her equally beautiful mother with a no nonsense bob haircut. "We just know we do not want a pit bull."

3 Days Earlier
Westside, Youngstown, Ohio

The windshield wipers slapped back and forth as Linda Morrison made her way back to the shelter. She had gone to visit her niece's new baby, little

Allison. Linda loved her great niece but she'd always felt a bit despondent when a baby was born. She had a flash of memory of Kevin's face in her mind. Kevin came from a big family and she knew he would have made a great Dad. She allowed herself to remember the several procedures they tried to conceive but to no avail.

"We were fine, just the way were," she whispered under her breath. "Plus we had the boys," she continued referring to Kevin's brother's kids. They had always taken them everywhere when they were little. Linda thought allowed herself to think about Kevin a little longer and heart ached with the thought of so many memories. She would be 40 this year. She felt her eyes well up with tears. She had a long time to be alone ahead of her. She was lost in her thoughts and emotions when she looked up and realized the light ahead had changed to red. She slammed on her brakes and the tires chirped, bringing the car to a sudden halt.

The rain was coming down quite hard as Linda sat at the red light. She wiped a tear from her cheek and looked in the rear view mirror noting more and more crow's feet. She winced as if to make them more pronounced, stared at herself for a moment and then flipped the mirror away. She turned and focused straight ahead intent not to think about her upcoming birthday.

Just then something caught her eye in a driveway on the other side of the intersection. Two pink paws were sticking out from under the tire of an old car with a tarp over the collapsed roof two perfectly pink paws. Linda turned on her hazards as the light turned green. She coasted gradually through the intersection and came slowly to a stop in front of a two story wooden house that was painted green. The house was in pretty bad shape. The green paint was chipping from decades of neglect. One lonely shutter hung from a rust nail on the second floor.

Linda pulled her raincoat hood up over her head, checked the side mirror to make sure nothing was coming and quickly exited the car into the pouring cold rain. She jogged up onto the sidewalk and carefully bent down to look under the car. Linda had to get on all fours to see under the car. Cowering behind the right rear tire was a very wet and dirty but otherwise perfectly white pit bull puppy.

"Hiya..." she whispered. The puppy stared, wide-eyed at Linda and retreated as far back as possible behind the tire. "It's ok, you're ok," Linda gently continued to whisper. She knew she could not crawl under that car with that frightened pup so she carefully backed up a little and sat up. She noticed a chain wrapped around the front bumper. *"Oh my Lord,"* she said to herself. She stood up stretching her back and thinking what her next move should be.

"Hey!" came the loud gruff bark of a man's voice from the front porch, "What the hell are you doing?" he shouted through the cold, rain.

"There's a dog under this car," she shouted back through the sound of the now downpour. The bearded man laughed.

"You're a freakin' genius," he said sarcastically as he took a long draw on a cigarette. He paused. "What's it to you?"

"He's scared and alone. He has no food or water. Why is he under there?" Linda said feeling something between fear and courage.

"Not that it's any of your business," the man shouted, " but it's because he's coward."

"He's a coward?" Linda was starting to feel her ears get hot.

"I bought him for a guard dog and he's afraid of his own shadow!' bellowed the man laughing. I hit him with a golf club and he didn't even fight back." Linda's fists clenched at her sides.

"You hit him with a golf club?" she said angrily and slowly emphasizing each syllable.

"He didn't even bite it." The man with the stained hooded sweatshirt bent down and then held up an old nine iron menacingly. Linda began to realize she might be in the presence of someone quite dangerous.

"Why don't you let me take him with me?" Linda said, forcing herself to sound casual. "I will take care of him."

"Why don't you let me get my gun?" said the man narrowing his gaze towards her. He shouted again before she could answer. "You're on private property Sweetheart." Linda heard whimpering from under the car and her instinctively protective nature surfaced.

"Well sir, you can get your gun and I'll go get the police. Under Ohio Revised Code Chapter 959 you are in violation of the animal cruelty laws of the State of Ohio." She puffed up her chest as the rain soaked her. "Or, you can let me take this animal with me, you go back in your house and we don't go get the police and a warrant to search your property for any other evidence of animal cruelty....or other criminal activity," she stared at him directly. "Your choice," she added shrugging. This was not her first rodeo.

The man squinted at her as if he were calculating his options. He thought for a long time staring her down. He took a long drag of the cigarette.

"Take it. Stupid coward of a dog. Take it far away...but I tell you what," he spat loudly off the porch, "if I ever see it again I'll shoot it in the face." The man flicked his cigarette at her, turned, and went into the house slamming the door behind him.

Linda let out a sigh of relief and faced the old car. She was still dealing with a frightened, abused, neglected animal and she needed to be very careful. She looked at the chain around the bumper. How would she ever get him free? She trotted back to her car and opened the trunk. She didn't carry bolt cutters but she certainly wasn't going to leave that dog behind. She let out a heavy sigh as she rummaged around looking for anything that might do the job. *Nothing.* She sighed and reached up to close the trunk. She turned as it slammed and she let out a gasp. A large hooded figure was standing directly in front of her. Linda put her hands up to push him away.

"It's ok," said a gentle voice, "I'll help you." A young black man with bolt cutters stood before her, his white teeth shining as he smiled at her.

Linda's shoulders relaxed. "Oh thank God." She looked up at him. "You're a guardian angel." She took a deep breath and let out a grateful sigh.

"I've been wanting to help that poor little dog for a while," said the young man and Linda detected a slight accent, "I feed him sometimes at night when everyone's asleep. He needs to get far away. I've been wanting to set him free but I don't think he would get far. I'm so glad someone finally came. Come on, we better be quick."

The young man trotted over to the bumper and picked up the chain. He clamped down hard and grimaced as he pressed with all his strength. It took several minutes and Linda was getting worried. Finally, the chain snapped hard and clunked down against the bumper. Another whimper came from under the old car.

Linda grasped the chain and began to gently pull.

"No," said the young man, "his throat." The man lay down on his belly in the wet gravel. He reached under the vehicle. "Come on," he coaxed. She could see that he had hold of one paw. Linda held her breath hoping there wouldn't be any growling or sudden panic. Slowly and very gently the man pulled out the white pit bull puppy from under the back tire. He pulled the dirty dog onto his lap and cradled the puppy's head for a moment against his chest. Linda could see the chain wound.

"You go with this lady, she will take care of you." He said stroking the dog.

The young man very gently lifted the chain from the etched circular wound on the pup's neck. The puppy winced with pain. He worked each section so gently and the puppy seemed to steel himself to endure the pain.

Finally free of his chain, Linda reached for the puppy who was alarmingly limp.

"I don't know when the last time he had food or water was, *He's* been on the porch all day long." The young man pointed his head to the big two story house. The man must have been on the porch when she arrived. Linda hadn't even noticed him.

"Thank you." Linda gathered up the dog in her arms. She felt the urge to hug the young man. She resisted and they smiled knowingly at each other.

"Linda." Linda cradled the puppy as she awkwardly freed one hand. He took it in his.

"Elijah"

"Thank you Elijah."

She turned to her car. Elijah watched as she placed the limp puppy on the front passenger's seat. She trotted around as the rain grew ever heavy. She looked back to Elijah. They both looked quickly at the big green house. The bearded man stood in the window with the curtain pulled back and watched them both carefully. Linda hopped in, put the car in gear, smiled an unspoken final thank you to the man and drove off. She adjusted the rear view mirror she had flopped up previously and caught a glimpse of what was behind her. She saw Elijah turn and ascend the stairs to the house next door.

CHAPTER ELEVEN

County Dog Pound
Spring 2015

The county dog pound was full…again. The county dog pound was always full. The paint chipped from the mint green walls which housed rows of cold damp cages. The concrete floor was a chilly uncomfortable bed to 65 lost and abandoned dogs. Doors slammed constantly and the echo of men's voices could occasionally be heard over the recurring barks of desperate dogs. Every so often the place would be momentarily silent. The detectable fear lingered in the air even when the dogs were asleep. The dogs were never really asleep. Not the sort of peaceful sleep of a dog on his master's bed. It was a vain attempt to forget where they were. Their eyes squeezed closed as they tried to escape in their minds to an open field, a back alley…anywhere other than here. Every different kind of dog imaginable could be found in the dog pound but mostly they were pit bulls and terrier mixes.

Rich Wrigley opened the big steel door, entered the back room and pulled the door closed behind him making a loud slam. He walked down the long aisle of steel cages. The cages were all posted with signs displaying dates. A few had names but mostly the dogs were identified by the date they arrived.

Rich sighed as he reached the pen of a small brown terrier/boxer mix. The sign on the cage said FEMALE TERRIER MIX, YOUNG/NO ID. The dog had been brought in by someone who found her wandering. She had been there quite some time. She had no ID and no chip. She was very shy and sweet but no one had come looking for her. Rich was at absolute capacity at home as well as at work. The dog was all brown with 4 white paws as if she had been dipped in paint.

The dog was at the back of the pen with her back to the dog warden. She turned her head to see who was behind her. Rich adjusted his round wire-rimmed glasses and tried not to look in her eyes. It was these moments that caused Rich to wonder how he had gotten himself into this situation. It was, ironically his love of dogs that brought him to the dog pound all those years ago. Back then they used to call him Ricky. He was affectionately known as Ricky Wrigley because it sounded like Ricky Wriggly and he was always wriggling with one dog or another. He loved dogs. He wanted to help the lost, the abused and the abandoned. He wanted to educate people on the importance of spaying and neutering and the paramount importance of responsible dog ownership. The overpopulation of dogs was a huge problem.

It made him so angry that people neglected to spay and neuter their animals and they let them roam free impregnating female after female. Those people either had no idea of the suffering they were creating or they just didn't seem to care. It was his goal as a young volunteer at the dog pound to change the way people thought. To help people understand just what was happening to all those puppies. How he had become the county dog warden was one part mystery and one part bad dream. Now he was just Rich. Sometimes, during lighthearted occasions he was called Rigs. Rich ran a hand through his salt and pepper hair. He took a deep breath and entered the cage. The dog whimpered and retreated.

"I know girl," he whispered. "It's time to go." He slid a looped cord around the dog's naked neck. Rich's heart had never hardened in all the years he had been there. Inside he was still Ricky Wriggly. He'd had this argument with himself more times that he could remember. He had no choice and he knew it. No one was coming for her. She'd been there the longest and there was an ever growing line of new admissions just beyond the gates. The new admissions never ended, never lessened, never let up one bit. They just kept coming one after another. Lost, abandoned and abused.

Sure, there were good days when various rescue organizations would arrive cheerfully and take several of his charges on their "Freedom ride" to Angels or Pawz. He would see them sometimes on Facebook and his heart would sing with joy for each rescued and homed dog.

He'd pleaded with dog owners to spay and neuter. He'd lectured when anyone would let him. People would often laugh lightheartedly and say things like "I would never do THAT to him," or "I just never got around to it," or "Would you like someone to do that to you?" He'd heard a statistic once that 1.2 million puppies are born globally every day. Whether or not that was true he didn't know. What he did know was that far too many dogs never left the dog pound.

His heart ached in his chest as he gently tugged the cord. The little terrier resisted and whined. He hadn't wanted to but he had to use quite a lot of force to get her to the front of the cage and through the opening. He left the door of the cage open as he walked her down the aisle. It was these moments when the dog pound was silent. He wished it wasn't so quiet. He didn't say a word. He didn't look at any of the silent dogs. He led the small, female, young terrier mix through the big steel door that said Authorized Personnel Only and the door slammed behind him.

Mission Street Rescue

Linda Morrison was about to lose patience with the mother, father, daughter trio who had been scrutinizing dog after dog all morning. Linda had introduced them to a black lab named Blaze, a little brindle boxer mix named Abby, a foxhound named Dexter, even a little Chihuahua named Gonzo. They found something wrong with every single one and their complaints always had something to do with what the dog looked like. Linda tried to maintain a cheery attitude as she presented each one of her dogs. She loved them all and would have taken them all home if she had the kind of money she imagined these people had.

"Well," she sighed. "You haven't met Lucky. He's our newest arrival." Linda led them to the very last pen. The mother took one look.

"Oh no," she turned abruptly as her daughter approached. "No, Abigail, don't even look. He's not for us." She turned her daughter's shoulder and pushed her back toward the door. “I suppose you don’t have anything for us,” the mother snipped at Linda. Linda bit her tongue. She had 17 dogs. Seventeen.

"You might consider fostering," Linda said finally. "Fostering saves two lives, the one you foster and the one who gets his spot," Linda said convincingly but her suggestion was met with a blank stare.

Just then there was a commotion in the front of the shelter. Katie and Rachel Thompson burst through the front door causing the bells above the door to actually fling off the hook, fly across the room and land with a loud clang in the corner. Pete the parakeet squawked indignantly and extended his wings fully on his perch making a loud fluttering sound.

“Mrs. Morrison!” Katie shouted.

Linda dashed down the hallway leaving the snooty family in stunned silence in the dog room. Linda emerged to find Katie and Rachel panting in the front room.

"What is it girls?" Linda hurried up to the two girls, their faces flushed with excitement and fear. "What is it?" Linda stared at the cardboard box in Rachel Thompson's arms.

"Twinkle's kittens!" Katie was obviously out of breath and sounded as if she'd been running for her life.

"Ok, ok..." said Linda calmly as she peered over the top of the box. "Oh my. They're brand new.

"Yes," Katie said holding back tears. "Twinkle's only a kitten herself."

"Twinkle?" Linda raised an eyebrow.

"Katie's been taking care of a stray kitten. She named her Twinkle. She didn't even know she was pregnant and then suddenly..." Rachel paused and nodded her head down toward the box.

"Ok, well let's get them registered." Linda walked toward the counter where she had a scale and forms to fill out for processing new kittens.

"No," Katie pleaded desperately, "you have to hide them!" Linda spun around and looked at Katie. "My dad and Mr. Kennedy are hunting them." Katie couldn't hold back the tears.

"Hunting them?" Linda said unable to hide her shock.

"They're going to drown them. You have to believe me. I heard them talking." Katie broke down and put her face in her hands. "Twinkle is still out there, all alone. They're going to get her and we have to go away…to Oglebay…" her voice was muffled by her hands and her tears.

Linda went over to the little girl she had known since the day she was born. She lifted Katie's chin.

"Your Dad wouldn't hurt a flea." She brushed wet strands of hair from Katie's red face.

"I heard him. He told Mom." Katie sounded as if she'd finally run out of steam. Her shoulders drooped. "He said they were going to drown them in a bucket. He had a bucket. Mrs. Morrison you have to believe me." Linda shot a look at Rachel. Rachel shrugged and nodded.

Linda squatted down in front of Katie. “You listen here Katie Bug Thompson. No one is going to hunt, drown or harm in any way any kittens on my watch. You leave them with me. If your dad shows any interest in these tiny kittens he’ll have to come through me. Okay?”

Katie’s lifted her red swollen eyes to Linda. She let a tiny smile creep across her face and she threw her arms around Linda’s neck.

“Thank you. But, what about Twinkle?” Katie’s eyes filled again with tears as she hugged her.

“I’m sure that Twinkle is going to be just fine. You’d be amazed how well a cat can do. It sounds like Twinkle is a good friend of yours. If you’re going to Oglebay that means your Dad will be away too. How about if I keep an eye out for her and if I see her I bring her here... to her kittens?”

Katie nodded. “Ok,” she whispered almost without any sound at all.

Mission Street Rescue

Lucky whimpered in his sleep. He opened his pale blue eyes momentarily just enough to see the darkness. The shelter was very quiet at night. He heard the occasional snore of his neighbors but for the most part it was silent. He really didn't know how long he had been there but he was starting to feel very alone. Each day he watched families who would come in with children and he could hear them playing with puppies. He could barely see from his pen into the main room but he was able to make out people cuddling puppies and cheerfully agreeing to take one or even two puppies home with them.

People rarely came as far as the row of pens he was in, but when they did they took one look and him and turned away. The lady with the graying ponytail was nice to him but she didn't have much time. She would take him on lovely walks but they were always very short and she always put him back in the pen after a quick cuddle as she moved onto his neighbors. Lucky placed one pink paw over his face and tried to force himself to sleep. He had a distant memory of his mother's warm belly and the warm wetness of her tongue licking his head. His heart sunk. He rolled onto his side and curled up in a tight ball trying to make himself as small as he could.

"Hey little one."

Lucky heard a deep, raspy, female voice and opened one eye. "Come on. Come over here." It was the coming from the large female boxer in the next cage. "Come over by me. I'll keep you warm." The boxer was lying with her body pushed against the steel grates of the cage. Lucky stared for a moment at the enormous boxer with big brown eyes and a white blaze down her face.

"Come on. I won't hurt you," she said softly and convincingly. Lucky inched forward toward her. He longed for touch and couldn't resist the idea of curling up next to her despite the fact she could probably swallow him whole. Lucky ducked his head submissively and

crept, almost sliding on his belly, over to the boxer, his little white tail wagging back and forth while all the while maintaining its downward position. He circled twice trying to figure out how to get the closest and he flopped down letting out an involuntary exhale.

"You'll be ok," she said. The boxer's face and Lucky's face were side by side and so close to each other that if he looked sideways at her his eyes would cross. He leaned his head in as if to nuzzle her appreciatively with the top of his head. He briefly looked up at her from his sideways position.

"They call me Ginger," said the boxer and her long tail with a white tip made two loud thumps on the hard floor.

"I'm Lucky." His voice was high and squeaky. "I guess." The two dogs lie quietly next to one another and Lucky felt a tiny bit better in his heart. "Have you been here a long time?" he asked without looking at her.

"Yes," she said despondently, "I have." She moved her head back so she could focus and looked into Lucky' eyes.

"It's not all bad. She doesn't... well, she won't. Well, you'll be safe here. There are other places where you would not be safe so be glad you were brought here."

"Why?" Lucky asked naively.

"You don't need to know that now," Ginger said. Her eyes were like two glossy brown pools of water with fantastic brown eyelashes. Lucky stared at her and his tail involuntarily wagged.

"Why are you here?" Lucky asked. This little dog sure asked a lot of questions and Ginger hoped she would not regret offering to be of some motherly comfort. She blinked slowly as she looked into Lucky's perfectly formed face and speckled little nose. She sighed.

"Because..." she paused and stared into his pale blue eyes. "Because..." she couldn't seem to find the words. "Because..." The large boxer rolled onto her side and lifted her back leg and exposed her underbelly. She nodded for Lucky's to look down to her tummy. "Because of this," she said sorrowfully. Lucky stared at Ginger's belly and he felt his tummy flip flop. Her bare belly

exposed two rows of large, stretched, soft, pink and brown teats that seemed to take up the whole space.

"No one wants that under their Christmas tree kid." She dropped her leg swiftly as if she were suddenly ashamed of the condition of her body.

"That's ok," Lucky said tenderly. "You're still beautiful." He tried to nuzzle into Ginger despite the cold steel grid separating them.

"That's kind of you kiddo but the fact is no one wants to take me home. I'm worn out. Damaged goods. Too many litters. I've had four large litters of puppies," she paused and looked at him, "I don't even know where they are." She turned and looked wistfully into the darkness. "Eighteen of my own pups. Gone." She paused and then seemed to gather herself. She straightened her paws in front of her in sort of mini stretch. "I'm good now though," she said proudly. "I've had an operation so that I don't have to worry about more puppies. They do it for all the dogs and cats here."

"Even me?" Lucky's right ear perked up and his voice squeaked.

"Even you," said Ginger softly, "but it's a very good thing. You'll be glad. It means you never have to worry about your puppies being taken away or hungry or hurt by anyone."

Lucky shuddered and remember the man with the golf club. He lowered his head to the floor. "Yeah," he said as he blew out his cheeks. Lucky lowered his chin all the way down to the floor and rolled over onto his back feeling much more secure, almost forgetting where he was. He stared up at Ginger who was looking down the aisle protectively as if she'd heard something.

"Ginger?" Lucky said her name quietly. The giant boxer looked down at the upside down pup. "Can I stay here with you forever?" His tongue fell out one side of his mouth. He looked adorable and silly.

"Gosh kiddo, for your sake I hope not."

CHAPTER TWELVE

Wethersfield, Ohio
Spring 2002

The little collie puppy woke up from a deep, exhaustion induced sleep. He lifted his head and looked out into the forest. The bright moon seemed very close as it hung low in the night sky and illuminated the whole forest. The scruffy little puppy could feel his heart beating in his chest. Crickets and other insects vibrated all around him. It had been several days that he had been lost in the puzzle of pastures and woods. He had spent a night in the forest but there were a lot of scary noises in the woods. He was frightened and lonely and he desperately wanted to get out of the dark wooded abyss.

His belly growled and ached with hunger. He was thirsty and hadn't found much food or water at all. He started to wonder if the man in the stocking hat was ever coming back. His brown eyes searched the moonlit woods. He walked forward and strained to see in the dark. He heard a far off howl and his ears craned to tune in the sound. He froze. All movement stopped. He waited. The howl faded away and the puppy again walked forward. He stumbled into a stump in the dark. He put his front paws up on the stump and lifted his head and neck, peering out through the trees. He saw a clearing! A tiny bit of hope swelled up and he used what little energy he had to climb out over the brambles. He excitedly burst out into the clearing. It was a vast meadow. No man in a stocking hat come to get him, just more open fields of nothing to eat or drink. He was lost. He had no idea where he was.

The puppy lifted his snout up high to the heavens and let out a long howl. A howl like the one he had heard in the distance. He wondered if someone else was lost out there in the chilly maze of meadows.

Suddenly, he felt the urge to bolt. Maybe if he ran as fast as he could he would get back to the place where he had last seen the man. Maybe he should just trust his intuition and just run where his paws led him as fast and as far as he could run. He hoped against all hope that his senses would guide him back the way he came. His breath was heavy as he began to charge through the field. His nostrils made moist trickles as the cold night air hit his snout. Small puffs of white steam emerged in repetition as if he was a small steam train. He panted and grunted, occasionally barking as he ran blindly through the long grass making a winding path of flattened hay behind him.

Chalet Number 5 - Oglebay, West Virginia
Easter weekend 2015

Katie Thompson's family had driven to Olgebay in an awkward silence. Katie and Rachel had been oddly quiet the entire afternoon. Katie's mother thought that surely she must have flunked her algebra test. She was usually open to discuss things like that but seemed to be completely closed off these days. Something was definitely going on but neither David nor Stacy Thompson wanted to press the girls. The young couple just wanted to enjoy their Easter weekend as a family, as always.

The Ford Explorer crunched onto the gravel driveway at Chalet Number 5. Number 5 was a tradition for the Thompson family and normally upon arrival the girls would have been chattering with greater enthusiasm the closer they got. By the time they got this far Rachel and Katie would have been bursting at the seams and scramble out of the car in a giggling race to the dark brown and stone A-frame lodge.

The gravel crunched again as the vehicle came to rest and David turned off the engine. He looked back hoping to find the girls asleep. His gaze was met with two blank stares from the backseat.

"Right," said Stacy enthusiastically, "we're here."

Katie looked up at the chalet's chimney as smoke bellowed gently from the stone structure. She sighed and tried not to think about Twinkle.

"Looks like they've started our fire for us. Isn't that nice?" David asked anyone who would answer.

Stacy obliged. "Sure is," she replied cheerfully. David turned his attention to the backseat.

"Grab your bags girls," he continued sounding forcefully cheery.

Katie and Rachel quietly exited the car and went around to the hatch at the back. David popped the button to release the hatch. He looked warily at his wife. "This can't all be hormones?" he said with a sigh.

Stacy shrugged and reached her hand towards him. She squeezed his hand in hers and forced a smile.

"She'll be fine once we get her on a horse." She tried to sound confident. But she wasn't confident. She was sure something was going on with Katie and now possibly Rachel. A mother just knows. She suspected Katie had been sneaking out of the house. She couldn't put her finger on it but she suspected her daughters had been lying to her about something.

Katie threw her backpack up on her shoulder and forced a smile at her sister. Rachel smiled back.

"Let's just have some fun ok?" she winked at Katie. "Everything will turn out fine."

Katie followed her older sister up the steps of her favorite chalet. She thought about the stables and the horseback riding. She thought about the lovely heated swimming pool. Her heart lightened a little bit and she felt a twinge of familiar excitement at the sheer fact that she and her family were there, at her favorite place.

She blew out her cheeks and sighed as she looked up and focused momentarily at the gray haze above them. Then she noticed something. They sky was moving. The sky was falling. It was snowing in April!

"Is that snow?" she asked, looking back at her father who was carrying some bags up the steps behind her.

"Yes it is Katie Bug. Good thing we got here early. They say we are in for a one, big, final nor'easter." He sounded way too excited. "We'll be super cozy in our chalet on a hill though right Sweetheart?" He pushed past her with both arms full of groceries.

We will be, thought Katie, *but what about Twinkle?*

CHAPTER THIRTEEN

THE TERMINAL

The little brown terrier mix with 4 white paws opened her eyes. She looked out across a beautiful, lush, green meadow. This didn't look anything like the noisy cold county pound. A thick mist hung in the warm air as if there had just been a rain shower. The dog stood in stunned silence as she took in the beauty. She'd never seen anything so beautiful. Butterflies danced across the sky and she could hear a babbling stream. She licked her lips and walked carefully toward the noise of the stream. Her head moved from side to side as she sniffed her way to a beautiful crystal blue stream of water. She leaned her head down and took a long lap of the perfectly clear blue water. It was sweeter than anything she had ever tasted. She lingered looking at her wobbling reflection in the water. She took another long drink. The water was so nourishing and she could feel her strength returning. She lifted her head as the water dripped from her mouth and she suddenly turned to the side. She gasped as she saw a face staring back at her.

"Hello there!" The old dog had a deep but very friendly and comforting voice.

"Hi." The little dog's voice was timid and almost inaudible.

"I'm Sid," said the old dog. The brown terrier mix just stared in silence at the warm eyes of Sid. She looked so sad and Sid's heart broke for her.

"So…what's your name?" he continued encouragingly.

"I don't have a name." The little brown terrier with the sad eyes tilted her head slightly.

"No name? Well, then you SHOULD have a name." Sid moved in closer. "Do you have any ideas?"

"No," the little dog said, and it was breaking Sid's heart. "Nobody ever gave me a name," she whispered.

"Hmmm…" Sid sat down and lowered his head to be at the same level. "I'm sorry to hear that." Sid's eyes were warm and wise. "I had a human. His name was Joe. Joe took care of me my whole life. He named me Sid. He loved me and shared his life with me before he died. Joe used to say that things that were beautiful were "Bella". I am going to call you Bella." The little dog could feel her face flush with warmth. No one had ever called her beautiful before.

"Bella?" She said her own name for the first time. She liked it. Sid could see he was making some progress and it made him very happy.

"So Bella, are you coming with us?" He tilted his head and looked deeply into her eyes. Bella was confused.

"Where are we going?" Bella asked naively.

"Up," Sid said coolly.

"You want me to go somewhere with you?" Bella had never been invited anywhere before.

"Yep, sure do! Up the rainbow!" Sid wagged his tail. "Joe's already up

there and since you don't have a human he can be your human. I'm happy to share him and he will absolutely love you. He lets me eat spaghetti. Do you like spaghetti?"

Spaghetti was lost on Bella and she looked at Sid suspiciously. "Where are we Sid?"

Sid puffed out his chest. "We're at the terminal Sweetheart."

"The terminal?" Bella asked.

"Look, beautiful Bella, I don't have an awful lot of time to explain because it will be here soon but you just trust me ok? You come with me and everything is going to be just fine. There will be a million rainbows if you want to wait for the next one but I'd like you to be on this one with me, ok?"

"What's a rainbow and why would you care about me?" Bella had never had a friend before.

"Well, for one thing I'm a border collie and it's my job to make sure that everyone stays together. The second reason is that I've been assigned to herd this terminal."

"I don't understand," said Bella.

"Do you have any reason not to trust me Beautiful?" Bella shook her head.

"Ok, so listen..." Just then, Sid had a thought. "I have a job for you ok? Follow me."

Bella followed Sid out of the meadow and they stepped out onto a path. The path had a slight glow to it and Bella gazed in wonder as she saw all the other animals on the path. Sid led Bella to a Dalmatian with large spots and one large black eye.

Sid spoke slowly. "This is Patch. He's here because he ate something he shouldn't have. He's a bit mischievous. Bella, can you do a job for me?" Bella nodded. "Can you make sure Patch gets to the bridge? Just follow everyone else and you will see it. Make sure Patch stays in line. Can you do that?" Bella nodded enthusiastically. "Thank you my friend. I'll see you at the top ok?"

Bella nodded not really sure what Sid was talking about but she was happier than she had ever been and she felt a great sense of purpose, something she had never felt before.

"Come on Patch, stay with me," she slid in next to the little, black and white spotted puppy whose tail was wagging furiously.

"Come on everybody!" Bella shouted to the ones at the back, "It's this way!" A Shetland pony let out a loud neigh and a parakeet flew past Bella's face with a whoosh. A turtle crawled slowly along. Two cats playfully trotted occasionally bounding over each other. The animals all chatted excitedly as they moved forward. Bella heard Sid's bark at the back of the crowd and then in the meadow on each side. He seemed to be everywhere.

Suddenly there was a bright light ahead. A whole mix of different colors washed over all of the animals on the path. The rainbow gently landed on the ground and the animals were all stunned momentarily by the magnificence. Bella heard Sid's bark at the front and the animals began to load one by one onto the rainbow. They easily walked, almost floating up the colorful bridge. Bella reached the base of the rainbow and helped Patch on. Sid barked a grateful bark and ran to the back. Bella and Patch ascended the rainbow in all its glory. The rest of the animals loaded one by one until they had all boarded the rainbow bridge.

Sid's wise eyes scanned the meadow for any sign of life. He barked and listened. He barked again. He thought he sensed something moving. He looked down to see two little dwarf hamsters.

"Sorry, we can't reach," they squeaked with their little paws waving.

"That's what I'm here for," said Sid, and he gently picked them up with the soft parts of his mouth and tenderly placed them on the rainbow.

The hamsters chatted excitedly as the scurried up. Sid scanned one more time. The rainbow was lifting. He perched on the end for a moment. He had done his job. There would be many more animals and there would also be many more rainbows but he'd cleared this terminal. Sid smiled to himself and bounded up the rainbow his heart bursting with excitement. He thought he heard someone call his name. He paused. He twitched with anticipation. He heard it again.

"Sid, come on boy!" He heard a familiar whistle. It was Joe.

CHAPTER FOURTEEN

Struthers, Ohio
Good Friday 2015

Twinkle shivered as she tried to wedge herself further inside the old stump. The little crevice she had found was barely big enough to fit her small frame and in that moment she was glad she didn't have her kittens with her. The old stump was at the corner of two streets in a small patch of woods.

Twinkle had often hidden in the woods while hunting and seen the neighborhood kids ride their bikes through the woods to the little convenience store on the other side of town. The stump was fairly hollow but the bark didn't provide much insulation. Twinkle had just reached the old stump and crawled inside when the cold white flakes falling from the sky and causing the ground to turn white.

She had encountered no other people or animals that whole afternoon or evening. It seemed the streets were deserted. She felt relieved that no one was looking for her but she felt very alone without her kittens and the kind little girl. She wondered if the little girl had been successful in hiding the kittens.

Twinkle curled herself into a small ball and covered her pink nose with her front paws. Her paws felt warm against her cold nose. The air grew ever colder as the sun faded behind the trees. The bare branches of the trees knocked against each other as the wind began to blow ever harder. The night seemed to become more and more unfriendly. She didn't hear any living thing. Not a mouse, not a mole, not even an insect was moving about.

Twinkle peered out into the darkness and felt a coldness and a loneliness she unfortunately had felt before. It was that familiar feeling she'd had before the little girl…she couldn't think about it. Her belly growled as she tried to force herself to sleep.

Sleep did not come. Twinkle finally lifted her head and smelled the air. She listened carefully as if listening to a distant voice. Her fear and loneliness now suddenly replaced with a new feeling. She could not shake the overwhelming urge to move. The night had fallen. It was completely dark and the air was colder than anything she had ever felt. Still, that feeling in her gut would not go away.

Twinkle stood up and turned around twice in the cramped little stump. She flopped down and felt the cold bark of the old tree scratch at her skin. She closed her eyes. The wind blew through the small opening of the stump. Twinkle's nose twitched as she smelled the cold wind upon her face. Her paws trembled with anticipation and cold. Twinkle sat up and listened again. The feeling was very strong. She felt as if she was just in the wrong place. She knew she had to leave and she knew where she had to go. She didn't know how she knew but she knew. She mustered up all her courage. She reached up on the bark of the old tree and did a quick claw sharpening. She stretched her back up as far as she could in the small space, took a deep breath and slipped quietly out of the opening of the stump and out into the frigid night.

Chalet No. 5
Oglebay, West Virginia
Good Friday 2015

Rachel and Katie sat obediently in the open-plan chalet living room playing checkers. The fire in the stone fireplace crackled and popped. The girls didn't say much. Stacy Thompson glanced over from the open kitchen at her daughters. The two girls seemed to have a new silent, unspeakable bond. Perhaps Katie had been able to talk to Rachel about her period more easily than she could her mother. Maybe it was just teenage girl stuff. Stacy had only had two brothers and no sisters so she really didn't know what sisterhood would be like. Stacy had been very excited at the second sonogram when she realized she would have two girls. She secretly hoped all throughout their childhood that eventually they would be like three sisters. That didn't seem very likely now.

Suddenly there was a whoosh of cold air from the side door of the chalet. David came in with a big armful of snowy cold firewood.

"What took you so long?" asked Stacy, as she motioned for the girls to help their Dad. Rachel and Katie helped their Dad unload the firewood into the cast iron basket near the hearth.

"I ran into Kim and Marty outside," he replied, dusting the snow off the sleeves of his coat and onto the kitchen floor.

"Oh?" said Stacy, trying not to look at the snow on the floor.

"Stace, you gotta hear this..." Stacy had been unwrapping chocolate and graham crackers for late night S'mores. She stopped unwrapping and focused on her husband's face. "Girls, listen to this." His daughters had resumed their game of checkers but stopped and looked at him. "Remember last year when Kim and Marty's dog, Shadow ran off?'

"Yeah," said Stacy, "that was awful. We searched for hours and hours. I felt so sorry for them. To lose your dog and have to leave without it."

"Well, get this. They got home to Pittsburgh and like four days later they got a call from the chalet rental office! Shadow was sitting at the backdoor of Chalet No 4!" He let out a loud jubilant laugh. "Isn't that great?"

Katie and Rachel stared at their father with their mouths open.

Stacy let out a little squeal. "That's incredible!"

David continued enthusiastically "I've heard that sometimes an animal will do that. Like, they will go to the last place they saw you and wait for you to come back." David shook his head in disbelief. "Apparently Marty let Shadow out the backdoor of the kitchen right before he ran off after the deer. I guess when he got tired of chasing the deer he came back to where he last saw Marty. Who knows how long he had been there, the chalet was empty!"

"Oh Darling, that's lovely. I'm so glad they found him." Stacy beamed at her husband.

"Yeah, he's outside right n…"

"I have to use the toilet!" Katie shouted suddenly. Everyone jumped.

"Ok Bug, calm down," David said coolly. Katie reached for her phone.

"With your phone?" asked Stacy.

Katie froze. "I have to poop!" Katie gave her Mom a wide-eyed look and ran to the bathroom. Stacy looked at David and shrugged. She looked at Rachel. Rachel was grinning.

"What is wrong with everyone?" Stacy sighed under her breath.

Katie slammed and locked the bathroom door. She opened her web browser and typed in Mission Street Rescue. She clicked. The signal was terrible in the mountains. It took forever but finally the page loaded. She scrolled down the yahoo listings. One, two, three…no it wasn't there. Then suddenly she saw it. Mission Street Rescue, Struthers, Ohio. There was no web link or webpage but just one listing with whitepages.com. Katie clicked the link, a little circle spun for what seemed like forever and finally loaded. She stared at the phone number. Mrs. Morrison wasn't that old was she? She didn't seem old. But was this phone number connected to one of those old phones like her grandparents had that hung on the wall and wasn't connected to anything but like, the phone? An 848 number could be anything. Maybe she could call the number and talk to Mrs. Morrison. Her mother knocked on the bathroom door.

"Katie, are you ok? Can I come in?"

"No!" shouted Katie, "I'll be right out!" She had one chance. She opened up her messenger and typed frantically with both her thumbs. IT'S KATIE THE OLD DESK BEHIND THE LAUNDROMAT IT'S THE LAST PLACE

SHE SAW ME. She stared at the text. Was it enough? Would she understand? Would she even get it? Was this going to end up going up some wire to an old, useless phone hanging in the back room of the darkened rescue shelter?

Her mother knocked again. "Katie, I'm worried about you." Her mother was not giving up.

Katie quickly hit the send button. She flushed nothing down the toilet and opened the door. She smiled at her mother as she pushed past.

"Katie..." said Stacy, "hands?" Katie looked down at her hands.

"Oh right. Sorry." She turned back, and washed her clean hands as her mother watched her carefully.

CHAPTER FIFTEEN

Mission Street Rescue
Good Friday 2015

It was nearly midnight by the time Linda Morrison had finished taking care of all of her animals. She didn't mind. She was usually there quite late. Tonight was particularly late because of the holiday and the volunteers having time off but she really had nowhere else to be and taking care of them gave her a sense of belonging. She couldn't imagine her life without Kevin and also without all of her animals.

Linda carried a pile of newspaper to the back room and turned off the light. She returned to the front of the shop and wandered down the stacked cages of cats and kittens.

"All right kiddos. I'm heading home. It's really cold and awful out there tonight so just being glad you're in here." She talked to the cats as if they were people. "I'll be back bright and early. Don't spill your water ok guys?" She poked her finger through the bars of a couple of cats who were still awake and gave them a gentle stroke.

She bent down to the glass incubator and she heard her knees crack. She felt the heat lamp and adjusted it. The three, fluffy, brand new kittens the Thompson girls had brought in were curled up and sleeping quietly.

"I hope your Mom's ok out there tonight," she whispered. The kittens lightly snored and purred. "I had hoped I would see her today, but I'm sure we'll find her tomorrow. It's pretty cold out there..." Her voice trailed off. She feigned hope as if the kittens were awake or able to speak English. She knew her job of taking care of these brand new kittens would certainly be easier if she could find their lactating mother. Linda shot a concerned glance to the littlest gray one. The little male kitten was alarmingly skinny but he was very active so that provided some comfort as to his future.

Linda pushed on both of her knees to help herself up. Her knees creaked again and she let out a sigh. She walked back to the row of dog cages. She felt the familiar twinge of suppressed panic as she noticed that she was almost at full capacity. Her least favorite part of running the shelter was turning away homeless animals because she was full.

Linda walked down the aisle of pens. She stopped and smiled at the second to the last pen and her anxiety faded. The little pit bull puppy was curled up against the belly of Ginger, the old mama boxer. Ginger's paws encompassed Lucky completely. Linda had found them one morning sound asleep with their noses touching through the grate. She had walked them several times together and they seemed to have really bonded. She decided after observing them for some time to put them in the same pen and see how they did. They slept and slept all curled up together. She'd never seen dogs sleep so soundly. The best part was that the little pit bull had finally stopped shaking! Linda thought she had even noticed less sadness in Ginger's eyes. The old boxer had sort of adopted the little guy. Linda smiled at them and said her favorite word out loud. "Adopt," she whispered. The boxer's massive tail made two giant thuds against the large pillow. Linda looked down and Ginger was looking at her with one beautiful, big, brown eye. She looked so content.

Linda leaned forward and allowed the top of her head to rest against the door of the cage. She watched how the little creatures shared each other's body warmth and seemed to have synchronized their breathing. Linda marveled at how something as simple as touch can change things, even with animals. Lucky looked more relaxed than she had ever seen him.

Linda thought about Kevin and how she longed to curl up against his warm chest and listen to his heartbeat. It felt like forever since she had felt him. She thought about the impending snow storm and remembered how they loved a good cozy night. How they used to take hot showers together on a night like tonight. Sometimes they would go straight from the hot shower to their bed and sometimes they would curl up in warm pajamas by the fire. Linda longingly remembered Kevin's touch as he would towel dry her hair and comb out all the tangles. She longed for his touch. She missed him and sometimes it really, really hurt.

Linda was suddenly snapped out of her daydream by an unexpected vibration and ping of her iPhone in her pocket. It made her jump. It was late. She pulled her phone out of her pocket and stared at the screen. She didn't recognize the number. *Who in the world would be texting her at this time of night?*

CHAPTER SIXTEEN

Mission Street Rescue
Good Friday 2015

The shelter was dark and quiet except for the howling wind outside. The April storm was powerful and record breaking. The shelter animals were acutely aware of the weather outside and were very grateful for their refuge. The animals had all been peacefully asleep for hours when suddenly Lucky opened one pale, blue eye. He purposefully wiggled his body against Ginger's warm belly. She opened one sleepy, brown eye.

"What?" she whispered.

"I have to pee," whined Lucky.

"Why didn't you go at last call?"

"I did," his voice cracked, "I have to go again." Ginger let out a big sigh and Lucky felt her warm breath puff across the top of his head.

"Hold it," she said sleepily and her lips relaxed and drooped against the pillow. She snored lightly.

"I can't!" Lucky sounded desperate. Ginger gently lifted her massive head and looked down at Lucky's wide eyed stare.

"Over there, by the door. There's paper. It's ok to go on the paper. It won't splash too much and the lady takes it away first thing in the morning. It's sort of only for emergencies. Is this an emergency?"

Too late, Lucky was already up and on the paper by the door. The only sound in the whole place was the tiny but surprisingly powerful stream of puppy pee hitting the paper. Lucky trotted back to Ginger's warm body.

"Better?" she nuzzled him back into his nest by her belly. He nodded and put his chin on the floor looking up at her. Ginger sleepily continued, "Don't drink so much water before bed..." she drifted off and Lucky squinted at her in the darkness. The little pup closed his eyes and tried to go to sleep. He was

only still for several moments. He fidgeted. He sighed. He got up and turned around twice, letting out a loud sigh when he plopped back down. He was wide awake. Ginger squeezed her eyes shut.

"Ginger?" Lucky whispered in the dark, "Are you still awake?" The giant boxer let out a long sigh.

"Yes, of course I'm awake with all your wriggling!" she said with exasperation.

"Well," Lucky continued carefully, "The other day, you said the lady wouldn't...well, you said there were other places where we wouldn't be safe. Is someone coming to take us away? Is someone going to take us to another place where we aren't safe?"

"Oh," Ginger mumbled sleepily, "No, don't worry about that."

"Oh," said Lucky quietly, but Ginger detected the fear in his voice. She thought about his chain wound and the bruises he had on his legs when he came in. She lifted her head and straightened her legs in front of her and

slowly lowered herself placing her head on top of her big brown and black paws. She adjusted her head so that they were nose to nose. She stared into the little puppy's eyes. She thought about all of her own puppies that had been taken from her. She looked at Lucky and swallowed the lump in her throat.

"Well, the thing is there's only so much room in the world for dogs...and cats...and hamsters...and, well you get the idea. So there are places...NOT THIS PLACE," she said reassuringly, "but there are places sometimes called "the pound" where you go in but you don't come back out," she looked away. "I've seen it."

Lucky gasped and Ginger's head snapped back as she looked down at the scared little pup as if she'd said too much. She had already considered she'd said too much a few days earlier and wished she'd never brought it up thinking she may have scared him.

"That's terrible," Lucky said, and his eyes were sadder than anything she had ever seen. "Were you at one of

those places?" He stuttered as he asked the question. Ginger nodded.

"I was. But I was rescued and brought here. Not everyone is as lucky...Lucky." She playfully bumped his nose with hers.

He didn't look any less sad or any less scared. She nudged him into her belly with her nose and one front paw. "You lie down and close your eyes and I'll tell you a story." Lucky slid in next to her and curled up in Ginger's warm abdomen. He could feel the protrusions on her tummy that had fed so many little mouths. He loved her teats. They made him feel secure. He didn't think they were any problem at all.

Ginger laid her head behind Lucky's head and whispered in his ear.

"There's a journey that we will all take one day." Lucky listened carefully. "There's a wonderful destination at the end of the journey and it doesn't matter how you get there. One day we will all come to a clearing. You and I won't get there for a long time but one day we will see every color we have ever seen all

together. There will be a great open meadow and the sun will be shining more beautifully than you've ever seen. We will have no pain and no sadness. There will lots of food and water, and balls to chase and TREATS," her voice went up a pitch, "and lots of friends to play with..."

Lucky closed his eyes and painted the picture with Ginger's words in his mind.

She continued, "Old animals will be made young again and hurt animals will be healed." Her voice sounded like a sweet melody to Lucky.

"We will see a bridge. The bridge will be more beautiful than anything we have seen before. We will only be able to see the beginning of the bridge but we will know exactly where to go."

Lucky's thoughts drifted off as he sleepily imagined a colorful bridge. Ginger continued to speak more quietly now. "Even those dogs and cats...and birds, and hamsters and even turtles... even those who don't make it out of the pounds or the animal hospital or if they die of old age; it's ok, because we all get to go up the Rainbow Bridge." Lucky smiled in his dreamlike state. "We will all go up the Rainbow Bridge and we will be with all of those who went over before us and sleep, eat and play until everyone else comes over," she paused. "Doesn't that sound nice?"

Lucky's body completely relaxed. She nuzzled him as he snored. Ginger lowered her chin and the giant boxer's thoughts drifted off to an open meadow full of little, brown puppies. She was glad he didn't ask her how she knew this. She didn't know herself. She joined her puppies in the meadow in her mind and she slipped into a deep sleep.

Chalet No 5, Oglebay
O' dark thirty Easter Saturday 2015

Katie drifted in and out of sleep. The wind howled outside and occasionally a big gust made its way down the big stone chimney. All the Thompson's chalet neighbors had been talking about what a massive record breaking storm they were having. It was an even bigger news topic than Shadow's miraculous homecoming. Katie didn't watch the news. She didn't look at her radar weather app. She did, however go to see Shadow. She kept her distance but she needed to see him to know that it was real. That he'd really gone back to the last place he had seen Marty. She said a prayer for her little furry friend and waited.

Everyone had gone to bed and Katie had just nodded off when she felt someone nudging her. Katie opened her bleary eyes and lifted her head just off the pillow.

"Huh?" She stared at the figure sitting on the bed trying to make out who it was.

"Katie, your phone buzzed," Rachel whispered, as quietly as humanly possible.

"It did?" Nothing was registering. "Oh," she plopped her head back on the fluffy white pillow.

"Bug," Rachel shook her again. Suddenly Katie sat straight up in bed. Her head snapped and she stared at Rachel, her green eyes even bigger than normal.

The two sisters sat in silence on the bed and Katie swiped her phone. She entered her 4 digit code and the phone came to life. The yellow envelope message icon had a red bubble with the number 1 inside. Katie looked up at her sister and took a deep breath. Rachel nodded her approval to continue. Katie pressed the envelope icon. It was a number she didn't know. There was no message. Her heart sank in her chest.

"Open it," said Rachel quietly. Katie sat paralyzed and stared at the number. Rachel reached down onto her little sister's phone and tapped the paperclip icon on the message bar.

The screen flipped and a picture slowly loaded. The two girls stared in disbelief as tears of joy ran down their cheeks. Three little gray and white kittens snuggled shoulder to shoulder in the incubator at the Mission Street Rescue and curled gently around them with her perfect pink nose and a detectible smile was Twinkle. She was a little bit wet but the heat lamp was warming her nicely. Her kittens were all latched onto her belly. Twinkle looked warm and content and the girls knew she was safe and sound.

The wind howled outside and the two sisters hugged like they had never hugged before. Rachel was almost embarrassed by her reaction but she knew her little sister was growing up. It had been her quick thinking that had saved Twinkle from certain death that frigid night. Perhaps her Mom and Dad weren't the only ones that weren't quite ready for Katie Bug to grow up.

McDonald Farm
Wethersfield, Ohio
Spring 2002

"Come on Cass! We're going to be late for the movie!" Claire Murphy shouted from the passenger seat of the 1994 Dodge pick-up. Cassandra McDonald trotted down the front porch steps of the old farmhouse pulling a zippered hoodie around her.

"It'll be all commercials in the beginning!" Claire shouted back.

Claire Murphy and Cassie McDonald had been best friends as far back as they could remember. Growing up in rural Ohio meant having very few close neighbors and Claire and Cassie had grown up on neighboring farms. They were two of only six girls on the whole school bus route and, as they were normally seated alphabetically they were usually desk neighbors as well. Their allegiance was galvanized in the first week of kindergarten when Claire had punched Doug Hughes right in the nose for his relentless teasing of Cassie and her family's last name. It was bad enough she lived on "Ole McDonald's Farm" but her parents' sense of humor made the situation much worse by actually naming their dog "Bingo". The girls were in their senior year of high school and Bingo had long since gone over the rainbow bridge but their bond was as tight as ever.

Cassie put the pick-up in first gear and waved at her Dad as she drove past the barn and out onto the road. The sun was just setting on the horizon and the chilly night air was closing in. Claire reached down and turned on the heat. She fiddled with the radio knobs. They were a good 20 minutes from home by the time Claire got any radio reception and even that was mostly static. Cassie's antenna had snapped off one night when Claire lost her footing in the mud and reached for something to catch her. The antenna snapped right off and sent the girls into fits of hysterical laughter. Fits of hysterical laughter was their very favorite state of being.

"I can't get any signal!" Claire exclaimed in a very loud, very bad English accent. Cassie giggled.

"See if you can find Tom Petty and the Heartbreakers or the bloody Beatles," she responded in an equally terrible English accent.

"Don't you find it terribly awkward to drive in silence?" Claire drew out the word awkward which was one of their favorite words.

"I do find it terribly, terribly awkward…" Cassie turned her head to look at Claire and drew out the word even longer.

"Look out!" shouted Claire suddenly. Cassie turned back to see something dart out from the long grass of the pasture and into her headlights. She slammed on the brakes making a loud chirping sound. But it was too late. Her front bumper hit the object and punted it out into the beams of her headlights on the road. It was a puppy.

"Oh no! Oh God! Oh No!" Cassie's eyes filled with tears. Claire reached for the door hand and got out. She bolted out of the truck and ran to the little dog. She bent down to see a very skinny little collie mix lying in the road.

"Cass! Come quick!" Cassie was frozen in horror behind the steering wheel with her hands over her face. "Cass look!" The little dog's tail was smacking against the hard asphalt of the road. "I think he's ok!" Claire was shouting to Cassie over the hum of the running truck engine. Cassie could not hear her.

Claire reached down and ran her hand all along the little dog's head and neck, down his spine and to the end of his tail. His tail never stopped wagging. She felt each one of his legs and moved them gently. He started to lift his head and looked back at Claire.

"It's ok, shhhh…" she comforted him as she continued to assess his condition. She moved all of his body parts very carefully and reached under his head. No blood, nothing seemed to be broken. He seemed to be just fine. She reached a hand under his side and drew him to her. She very gently and carefully picked him up and cradled him like a baby. His front paws were limp but his tail was a whirlwind of movement. The puppy leaned his head up to Claire and licked her cheek gently with his warm soft tongue. Claire carefully carried the puppy over to the driver's side window. She gently tapped the window.

Cassie pulled her hands away from her face and slowly, as if in slow motion she looked over at her friend. Her eyes were wide with disbelief. "Is he hurt?" she asked rolling down the window.

"I don't think he is Cass. I think he just rolled." Cassie reached an apprehensive hand toward the puppy. Claire and Cassie were avid animal lovers and to think that Cassie could ever have hurt a puppy would have devastated both of them. The puppy's tail never stopped wagging while they looked him over.

The girls brought the puppy inside the cab of the truck and examined him more carefully. The more they cuddled him the more active and alive he became. Soon he started an excited whimper. His whole body was wiggling by the time the girls had closed the doors and Cassie put the truck in gear.

“He’s so skinny,” said Claire as she cuddled the little pup.

“He's a stray, don't you think?" The little dog's bushy tail wagged enthusiastically.

"Yes, I would say he's a stray. Well, it looks like the little chap could use a hamburger!” The loud English accent had returned.

“To Burger King, McDonald!” Claire exclaimed. That joke never got old to Claire.

The two girls had forgotten all about the movie. They knew they couldn’t keep the dog but they were off to spoil this little dog and spoil him good.

The girls spent the evening playing with, feeding and generally spoiling the little dog. He was very hungry and very thirsty and he lapped up anything they offered him. It was very satisfying. The time for the movie to be over had passed and the girls were avoiding the obvious looming problem.

"Claire?" Cassie's voice was cautious

"Mmmm?" Claire was rubbing her face all over the little dog's head.

"What are we going to do? I mean later? Like, we can't take him home." Being farmers both the Murphy and McDonald families were constantly being asked to re-home strays and animals that needed a new place to live. Their fathers were adamant that they were not to bring home any animals whatsoever. The sides of Claire's mouth dropped as she held the puppy's face in her hands. She frowned at him.

"We can't take him to the pound. They might kill him in the pound," she mouthed the words so the puppy didn't hear. Cassie's blood ran cold as she stared at her worldly friend. Although they were the same age Cassie had always thought of Claire like a big sister. She knew things about the world and about life that Cassie just didn't seem to know.

"Really?" Cassie said naively.

"Sometimes...they have to. It's just the way it is. Too many dogs in the world. It's so sad," Claire hoisted the dog's front paws up so he was standing on his hind legs on her lap tail wagging. She stared into the little dogs soulful brown eyes. "You need a name," she searched the little dog's face. "You look like royalty to me. Do you think he looks like royalty?" She turned the little dog toward her friend. Cassie gave the little dog a once over.

"Yes. The Earl of Winchester," she giggled at her own exaggerated accent.

"The Duke of Edenborough," Claire said with the poshest of accents. She paused. The girls locked eyes and had a "*best friend no need for words moment*".

"Ok, Duke," she grinned at Cassie. "Here's the deal. We can't take you to the pound because....because they don't have any room. So, we are going to take you to the Animal Welfare League." Claire spoke confidently.

"Animal Welfare League?" Cassie said inquisitively.

"Yes, it's all volunteers, it's not far from here and it's a no kill shelter," again she mouthed the last few words and covered the dog's ears this time. "We just have to pray they aren't full. If they are full I don't know what we will do," Claire's voice faded off as she gazed into Duke's brown eyes.

"Well then let's pray," Cassie said confidently. The two girls had been raised in Christian homes where prayer was something that was open and frequent. So they did. The two girls sat in the truck with the little puppy that had stolen their hearts and part of Cassie's headlight, and they prayed that they would have room for Duke at the Animal Welfare League.

CHAPTER SEVENTEEN

Mission Street Rescue
Late Spring 2015

Lucky and Ginger were curled up together on the cool concrete floor as the afternoon lazily passed by. The two dogs had become extremely bonded with one another over the past few weeks. Ginger had never been so happy and full of love in all her life. Lucky felt secure and loved which was also a new experience for him. Ginger's belly puffed up as she took a deep breath and stretched out her legs. Lucky followed suit mimicking his friend and he let out a smaller, quiet sigh.

Suddenly Ginger's right ear twitched and she opened one eye. Someone had come in the front door. Ginger and all of the animals were used to the sound of the chimes above the front door but for some reason Ginger did not have a good feeling about whoever had come in.

Voices echoed through the shelter and they could hear Linda speaking with a man. The conversation sounded pleasant enough but Ginger had a bad feeling. The light flickered on in the dog wing of the shelter and Linda appeared, accompanied by a man in a baseball hat and a green t-shirt. They strolled down the lines of pens and the man peered into each cage as if he was on a search for something in particular. The two of them stopped in front of Ginger and Lucky's cage. The man bent down and peered past Ginger straight to Lucky who was now behind her.

"That one," he pointed at Lucky. Linda looked at the man for an uncomfortable amount of time.

"That's Lucky. I rescued him myself from a bad situation," she peered at the man.

"Can I see him?" asked the man without looking at Linda.

"Well, the thing is they are quite pair bonded. If you meet Lucky you really should meet Ginger." The man looked at Ginger quickly and dismissively.

"Nah, just the little pit bull," the man said flatly.

"Ok, well I guess you can meet him…we just would really not want to split them up…"

"Just the pit bull," the man interrupted her. Linda reached for the latch and turned it. She kept one eye on the man. Ginger stood protectively over Lucky. Linda gently nudged her aside.

"It's ok girl," she whispered to Ginger. Lucky cowered behind Ginger before being plucked up and carried out by Linda. She handed Lucky to the man. Ginger began to whine.

"He's pretty small. But I suppose he'll do," said the man examining the dog.

"Do for what?" Linda asked suspiciously.

"For a family pet," the man stammered and Linda felt uncomfortable. "The wife said not to get one that's too big," he continued as if trying to recover.

"Wouldn't your wife like to meet your family pet before you bring it home?"

"Oh, nah…she trusts me. So, what's the fee?" he reached around to his back pocket for his wallet. Ginger let out three loud barks and raked one massive paw against the steel grid of the cage. She lowered her head and sniffed vigorously at the bottom of the pen trying to smell the man. She scratched and pawed furiously where the floor met the cage.

"Well," said Linda boldly. "It's not just the matter of an adoption fee. It's a process Mister...?" her words hung in the air.

"Jones," he said almost too quickly.

"Mr. Jones, come this way and we will fill out an application and we will consider whether we think you would make a suitable home for our Lucky," she rubbed the top of Lucky's head and winked at him. Linda, Mr. Jones and

Lucky made their way down the aisle of pens and Ginger let out a long loud howl.

Linda stepped behind the shop counter where she kept all of her record and paperwork. She handed the man a clipboard and a pen. “You start working on this and I’ll just need to see some ID,” Linda had amazing discernment and she thought she knew how this was going to end.

“ID?” he said indignantly.

“Yes ID. Standard procedure,” she reached for Lucky. “I’ll just hold him while you get it out,” she reached over the counter and pulled Lucky from his grip before the man could think. Ginger’s howl was deafening. The man reached for his wallet shaking his head. A gray cat with bright green eyes jumped onto the counter and stared defiantly at the man.

“This is ridiculous,” he muttered under his breath. “It’s just a dog,” he handed Linda something from his wallet. “What’s wrong with that dog?” the man shot a glance back toward the pandemonium Ginger was causing.

Linda looked at the man's ID.

"I go by Jones," he said awkwardly. Linda took a deep breath as if to gather herself. When she looked back up at him she was shooting daggers with her eyes.

"I know exactly who and WHAT you are Mr. Zeigler," she drew out his name and spat it at him. "If you ever so much as darken my door again you will regret it," she continued shouting over Ginger's howling. "You disgust me and if I ever get a chance to bust your dog fighting operation I will see to it that you NEVER see the light of day again," she was coming out from behind the counter now holding Lucky protectively in her arms. "Now, you better get out of my shelter before I open that pen and let Ginger give you what you deserve!" Linda was shouting, her face was red and her blood was boiling.

"Whatever you crazy hippy....it's just a dog," he was backing up looking at Linda's rage filled face.

"GET OUT!" she hissed at him and moved toward the dog pens reaching one hand out. "Get out or I'll let them all at you!" The man shouted some obscenities and finally slipped out the door. The echo of the chimes hung in the silence. Ginger was quiet. Linda hugged Lucky close to her. He looked up at her and his tail wagged for the first time since the man had entered. She continued hugging him as she carried him back down the aisle of pens. She stopped and stared. Ginger was lying on her side. She wasn't moving. She didn't seem to be breathing. She looked as if she were dead.

"Ginger?" Linda said trying to control the panic in her voice. She reached for the latch. "Ginger?" she shouted this time as she opened the door. Linda squatted down with Lucky and gently placed him close to the giant boxer. Linda held her breath as she reached down to feel Ginger's body. Suddenly, the giant boxer opened one eye. She stared directly at Linda.

"Here," she whispered. "It's ok, he's here," she nudged Lucky toward Ginger.

The big boxer slowly lifted her head and her bloodshot eyes focused on the little white pit bull. Her tail suddenly smacked the concrete floor with great, loud thuds. Ginger began to cry. She jumped to her feet and began making long, loud whimpers. Her whole body wiggled as she licked Lucky all over. She licked him so hard that he fell over several times. She pawed at him with her giant paws and pushed him to the floor.

"Ok, ok," Linda giggled. "Don't hurt him," she gave Ginger long strokes on her back to sooth her. Lucky was lying where he had fallen over and Ginger curled her body around him. She licked him repeatedly on his little pink eyes and pink ears. Linda smiled at the two of them.

"Let's not ever do that again," she whispered and prayed in her heart for someone to come who would want to take them both. Linda gently and quietly backed out of the pen. She quietly closed the door and once again placed her forehead against the cold grids. She lingered, she thought about Kevin. She gazed at the dogs acknowledging in that moment, the sheer power of love and the happiness and heartbreak it can bring.

Animal Welfare League
Spring 2002

The rescue shelter was full of activity on a busy Saturday morning. The weather was just breaking which often meant an influx of new admissions. The sound of spring bird songs filled the air and a crisp breeze blew through the open back door of the rescue shelter. The freshly mopped floor smelled distinctly of bleach. A fox terrier sat quietly gazing out of his cage. A stout bulldog snored quietly in the cage next door. A small skinny collie dozed on a pillow at the back of one of many cages all stacked on top of one another. The sign on the cage read DUKE/YOUNG/COLLIE MIX/AVAILABLE.

The many volunteers bustled around cleaning cages and wiping down surfaces. The sound of scoops of food hitting bowls and running water filled the atmosphere. The lobby door opened and one of the volunteers entered accompanied by a young woman. She looked as if she'd been crying for days.

"Go ahead and have a look around. Don't open the cages but if you'd like to meet anyone just give me a holler and I'll get them out of you," said the volunteer wearing a navy blue Animal Welfare League t-shirt.

"Ok, thank you," said the young woman quietly as she looked on quite bewilderedly at the many cages. The volunteer walked back through the door and closed it behind her.

The young woman looked back at the closed door and then back at the room full of dogs. Every dog in the room was now barking. The dogs scratched at the cages as she walked down looking into each cage. The young woman wondered how all those dogs got there. *Was there no one to keep them? Were they all lost?* Her heart ached as she thought about her recently lost best friend. She knew that her family could provide a loving home for a new best friend but was she trying to replace him? E*ven if she wanted to how could she* *possibly pick from all of these beautiful dogs?* She wanted to open all the cages and just free them all. They just seemed so desperate.

She stopped and looked around helplessly. Her heart ached in her chest. She wanted to turn and run straight back out that door. *Maybe it was too soon. Maybe she wasn't ready for this.* She let out a long sigh and pulled a Kleenex from her pocket. Her pockets were full of wet Kleenex. *This definitely isn't helping my broken heart,* she thought.

She dropped her head helplessly and it was then that she saw a little face staring at her from the bottom row of cages. She paused and her breath caught in her throat. She slowly squatted down and was face to face with a skinny little collie. She was frozen still as she stared into his warm brown eyes. He wasn't barking. He wasn't making a sound. He just stared at her with those amazingly tender eyes. She recognized something in those eyes. Something she knew. She drank him in as she stared. All the sound around her seemed to fade away as they locked eyes.

Abruptly, she got up, turned and went quickly out the door. The little collie dog stared at the door as it slammed closed and slowly his front paws slid out ahead of him as he lay down, letting his chin land slowly on the concrete floor. He waited. The barking subsided. He let out a sigh and closed his eyes.

Suddenly the door opened and the young woman was back! She was now accompanied by not only the woman wearing the navy blue shirt but also a young man and a small boy. The barking resumed.

"Can we meet this one?" she asked excitedly as she pulled the young man by the hand to the cage that with the name Duke written on it. The young boy was also being pulled along by the man in a Cleveland Indians hat. The little collie, again sat in complete silence as they approached.

"Sure can. This little guy was found somewhere out in Wethersfield. We think he's about 12 weeks." The woman opened the cage and pulled the little collie out. "He's probably part collie part shepherd. Cute ain't he? He was brought in by two young farm girls who found him on the road. He could use a good meal or two and probably a good night's sleep somewhere quiet." The woman rubbed the collie between his fluffy ears and handed him to the woman. "I'll give you a moment or two to get to know each other. Give a yell if you need anything," she said cheerfully and went back through the lobby door.

The little family cuddled the scrappy collie dog. "Duke huh?" said the man looking deep into the dog's eyes. He took the dog in his arms and rolled him back into the crook of his elbow so that the puppy was belly up. The dog flopped his paws submissively and his tail wagged gently back and forth. "You sure could use some food." He felt the dog's belly and put his hand in the dog's mouth momentarily. He looked over to the young boy. "Come here son," he called and gently knelt down. He held the dog in front of the small child. "What do you think?"

The boy shrugged and grinned. He was covering his ears to block out all the barking. The sound was deafening. All the while he was talking to his son, the man was nonchalantly poking his fingers in the dog's ears while the woman simultaneously threaded her fingers through the dog's toes. The dog was extremely unbothered.

The couple locked eyes. The young man noticed that his wife's red, swollen eyes were looking a little less heartbroken. He stared lovingly at her. He smiled and raised his eyebrows. She gently nodded.

"Welcome to the family," said the man to the little dog. The woman let out an involuntary squeal, leaned forward and kissed him on the lips. The little dog craned his head up, tail wagging furiously and licked the woman on the chin.

"Eww," said the little boy laughing. The woman giggled and wiped away a happy tear. The couple stood up. She threaded her arm through the man's free elbow as he cradled the dog. She took her son by the hand and the family of four walked confidently out into the lobby gently closing the door behind them.

CHAPTER EIGHTEEN

Mission Street Rescue
Midsummer 2015

It was a busy Thursday evening and Linda had facilitated 4 adoptions. This made her very happy but, as is always the case, she had equal to or even more new admissions. Today it was 2 cats and 3 dogs. She had been stuck behind the counter most of the evening because of all the paperwork associated with the applications and the admission paperwork, not to mention the documentation that was necessary for all the microchipping.

Linda came out from behind the counter and looked around the room. She had a lot of work left to do. Katie Thompson was there of course. She was Linda's newest and most dedicated volunteer. It seemed that Katie did the lion's share of work anymore by herself.

She didn't seem to mind and she got to spend almost every day of her summer vacation with Twinkle. It was sort of a perfect situation because Katie's mom didn't have to worry about her during the day while she was at work. It was a win-win-win situation.

Twinkle was a bit of a celebrity. She was a shelter greeter and greet she did. She would meet all new guests at the door with a purr and gladly escort them throughout the place. She was adored by everyone who met her. She was about the most lovable cat anyone had met before. Of course, she could hold her own with the rambunctious puppies who tried to chase her. She wasn't afraid to sink a claw into a nose or use her powerful hiss to send them running for Linda.

Linda made her way back to the dog wing to change newspapers while Katie got the food ready. Linda walked around the corner to see a man standing in front of Ginger's cage. She thought everyone had gone. He must have been standing there for quite some time because he hadn't come in recently.

"Hello," she called out to him. Startled, the man jumped a bit.

"Oh. Hi." He said composing himself.

"Sorry, I didn't' mean to startle you," she smiled warmly.

"No, no. It's okay, I was lost in thought," he smiled at her shaking his head. The man looked back at Ginger and Lucky. "What's going on here?" he smiled at them standing with his hands deep in his pockets. His voice was very deep and Linda found it somewhat soothing. He had a slightly sunburned nose. He looked to be in his late 50's. He wore brown rimmed glasses and smelled of the outdoors.

"Well, Ginger's a very well-seasoned Mama. She's had many litters taken away and Lucky needed a Mama. He was abused and scared when I rescued him and they just took to each other. One morning I found them basically cuddling through the grates of the pens." Linda smiled at the two dogs lying side by side, always touching.

The man pulled his hands of his pockets and thoughtfully stroked his brown and gray beard stubble. His hands were worn and scarred like he had done a lot of hard work in his life. The skin around his eyes was wrinkled like hers. He looked older than he should look, like he had been through some hard things that had taken a toll but he looked kind and gentle. His voice was calming. Linda tilted her head to the side and stepped forward.

He turned to her. "Mike Adams," he said putting his hand out.

"Linda," she said smiling cautiously.

"The thing is Mike that these two really seem to need each other. I really want to find them a home where they can stay together. When we try to separate them they really don't do well. Do you understand?"

He turned to her and smiled knowingly. "Yes, I do," he looked first at Linda and then back to the dogs.

"We have lots of lovely dogs who are ready to go on their own if I can show you some of them?" she leaned toward the other dogs.

"I'm not interested in the others," he said smiling and gazing into the pen.

"Well, I'm sorry I won't split them up. I'm really sorry." She shook her head.

"Linda," He turned to her, "I'm interested in them both," he smiled warmly.

"Oh." Linda let out a long relieved sigh. "I see," she continued.

He looked up at the ceiling for a second. "You see, it's been 8 years since I lost my wife. Breast cancer…," He put his hands back in his pockets and looked at his feet as he shuffled them on the concrete floor. "And 6 years since I lost both of our dogs…both of them that same year." He lifted his eyes up and looked into Linda's eyes. "I don't want to be alone anymore."

Linda felt her tummy flip flop. She hadn't felt anything like that in years. "Oh," she said quietly.

"One day I just woke up and said enough is enough." His voice changed to a more optimistic tone. "I decided that I want to live and I want to share my life with someone." He turned his head back and nodded to Lucky and Ginger who were now standing at the door of the pen wagging their tails.

"I get that," said Linda now also looking at the excited dogs. There was a long uncomfortable pause. "You see, I'm a widow," she said softly. He looked down at her wedding ring and nodded. 'I know right?" she said with a nervous laugh. "Probably will have to take that off some time." Her voice cracked.

"How long?" he asked tenderly.

"Almost 6 years."

"Mmmmm," he gave one big nod of his head. "You'll be ready to start living again soon. Don't rush it," he said gently. "No one but you will know when you're ready. You certainly have your hands full here." He looked around at all the waiting faces.

"No doubt," said Linda.

"I think two are better than one because they don't get lonely." He nodded to the dogs. "Why don't you and me take these two for a walk and see how it goes..." He saw the look in her eye. "Between me and the dogs," he said reassuringly, recognizing that she might be misunderstanding. Linda smirked slightly and Mike winked at her.

"I guess there's no harm in that," she said shyly. "I suppose it's best if l go too since there are two of them. There's a nice little park just down the road. Let's see how it goes." she reached for the leads on the wall and handed him one.

"You take the big one ok?" she laughed.

"Oh, okay I see how this is gonna go," he chuckled.

Linda smiled and opened the pen.

Mission Street Rescue
Two days later

Katie arrived early in the morning and used her own key to open the front door of the shelter. The chimes jingled above the door as she entered.

"Good morning guys!" she said cheerfully. There was a distinct thud as Twinkle landed and ran toward Katie.

"Hi Sweetie," she said crouching down. Twinkle purred loudly and rubbed all over Katie's hands and bent legs nearly knocking her over. It always made Katie giggle when Twinkle did that. She was just so tremendously affectionate.

"Come on girl, we've got work to do," she bent down and picked Twinkle up. The small gray cat continued to purr even louder. Katie carried her furry friend behind the shop counter and flicked on the fluorescent lights. Twinkle slinked out of her arms as she lowered her to the counter. Katie set down her keys and brown bag lunch and headed for the dogs. They would all need to be walked first thing and then fed and watered and their paper changed. It was a never ending cycle.

Katie was on her third dog when Linda arrived. Linda was so very much enjoying Katie's constant help and volunteer service all summer. It was so nice to have someone to really share the burden and it also meant that sometimes she didn't have to get up before dawn. Katie really seemed to want to do it and she was much more reliable than some of the dog walkers who did or didn't show up from day to day. Linda had seen Katie change in the course of just a few months, from a little girl to a young woman.

"You ok with walking?" Linda asked from behind the counter.

"Yep," said Katie cheerfully.

"Ok, I'm going to go check on our new arrivals," Linda went into another room. A new litter of brindle mixed breed puppies had arrived the day before and Linda went about the business of corralling the puppies while she changed paper and filled the water and feed bowls.

The two ladies worked all morning on the physical labor part of running a shelter and by early afternoon they moved on to the other tasks. Linda was beginning to train her newest helper in the ways of the business side of running a shelter. They had unlocked the front door for business and turned the closed sign to open.

"This is our spay and neuter schedule..." Linda showed Katie some documents. Twinkle sat on the papers blocking Katie from looking at them. Katie giggled.

"I've got to see those," she said gently nudging the cat. Twinkle continued to purr and circle on the papers. The little gray cat lowered the side of her head down to the counter looking up at the women and allowed her body to flop completely on its side. She rolled over on her back and wiggled around on the papers.

"Oh my goodness Twinkle," said Katie. "You're ridiculous." Katie picked up Twinkle and placed her on one shoulder while she listened and studied the documents on the desk.

The women were interrupted by the jingle of the door chimes. A man wearing a Cleveland Indians baseball hat in his late forties walked in with a similarly aged woman and a teenaged boy.

"Good morning," Linda called out from behind the counter.

"Oh, good morning," said the man.

"What can we do for you this morning?" said Linda.

"Well, we think we are looking for a cat," said the woman.

"You think you are?" asked Linda inquisitively.

The man lowered his voice. "We lost both of our rescued dogs this summer and we might not be ready for a new dog but we think a new cat in the family might be a good idea," he said quietly.

"Oh, wow," Katie couldn't help her shock. "Both?"

"Yes," said the woman. "They died one month apart. But, they died of old age. They both had a wonderful life," continued the woman affectionately. Katie's chin dropped as she thought about how sad that would be. "We're healing but we have a 9 year old cat who isn't taking it so well," she said tenderly. "We thought a new friend for him might be a good idea," she moved forward and reached a hand out stroking Twinkle who was sitting on the counter. "Isn't she beautiful?" she admired Twinkle's pretty features.

"She's not up for adoption," said Linda quickly. "But all the cats and kittens in the cages are available. Well, most of them. Have a look around and if you want to meet anyone just let us know," she gestured over to a long line of cages.

"I'm going to have a look at the dogs, just out of curiosity." The woman pealed off to the dogs and the man followed her. The teenaged boy made a beeline for a cage containing a very small, somewhat skinny, gray kitten with green eyes and also a very large tabby cat. The gray kitten became very excited and trotted back and forth in the cage, his eyes locked on the boy. He rubbed his whiskers and cheeks against the bars and the boy could hear a loud purr.

The couple looked around at all of the animals asking many questions about the various ages and breeds of dogs. Linda answered all of their questions the best she could. She had more information about some than others. Katie's gaze was locked Twinkle who was now nuzzling the boy's leg and also on Twinkle's kitten. After some time Linda overheard the woman.

"I'm just not ready let's just get a cat today. We can always come back. Cats are a pretty seamless transition and I don't think I'm ready to give my heart to a new dog...yet," she shot her husband a smile.

"There's no hurry Love." He put his hand in hers and they walked over to the boy still petting the little cat through the bars.

"This one," the boy said confidently.

"This one?" the woman asked. "Why this one?"

"I just like this one that's all," he said poking his fingers through the bars and stoking the cat the best he could.

"Is he...she a kitten or is it just small?" the woman asked awkwardly. Linda joined the family near the kitten cages.

"He's technically a kitten, about 5 months old. He was the runt of the litter but he seems to be doing fine now." Katie looked up from her documents.

"His mother is actually right here," Linda picked Twinkle up and Twinkle and the little gray kitten purred enthusiastically.

"He's a miracle. He's her last kitten," Katie said trying not to sound desperate. Linda's breath caught in her throat as she felt Twinkle's soft fur.

"Yes, he is the last kitten. His sisters were both adopted." Linda knew the word "last" had more than one meaning because Twinkle had been spayed since arriving on that frigid April night.

"Can we see him up close?" asked the man. Linda set Twinkle down and opened the door. The kitten leaped out of the cage and into the boy's arm. He chuckled.

"Friendly aren't you?" he said while the kitten rubbed his head all over the boys chest until one of his ears was flipped back exposing perfect pink flesh, but he didn't seem to mind. The purr was astounding. It started with a small hum and then, as if the kitten couldn't control it, became like a locomotive barreling down the tracks.

"Shall we look around a bit?" inquired the woman of her son.

"No, I don't think so. "I like this one. " The woman lifted her eyes inquisitively to her husband. He shrugged and smiled.

"You sure?" she asked.

"Yes." The boy was resolute. The woman gazed at the kitten who was still purring loudly. She stroked him under his chin and he blinked at her slowly. For such a little guy he had quite a wide chest. His chest had a white patch as if he were wearing a vest or a suit of armor.

"Well then," she turned to Linda, "I suppose we would like to look into adopting this one," the woman said calmly. The man plucked the kitten from the boy's arms and sat on the bench.

"You guys go fill out to the forms. I'm going to have a look at this little fellow." The kitten's purr had not lessened and if it were possible it may be been louder upon the man's touch. The kitten bit the man on the brim of his Cleveland Indians baseball hat. "Hey, hey," he said chuckling and pulling the kitten away. "Watch the hat."

The woman took a clipboard from Linda and paused. Somehow sensing

Katie's bond with the cats, she looked over to her warmly.

"He'll have the very best life. I promise you." Katie fought back a partly happy/ partly sad tear. She nodded. "He'll have at least one big brother. He'll sleep on our bed. He'll have lots of toys and good food and we won't let anything happen to him ever," she said convincingly. "You can even come visit if you like," Katie's eyes sparkled for a moment.

"Okay, thank you," she said slightly more cheerfully.

The family was approved for the adoption and Linda let Katie microchip Twinkle's little kitten. When she was finished Katie crouched down holding the kitten close to Twinkle who had been roaming the shelter but was now at Katie's feet. Twinkle licked her son and purred. She nuzzled him but only for a few seconds. She looked up at Katie. She made her little hum/purr noise and slowly and quietly walked past Katie brushing Katie's leg with her body quite hard.

Katie looked at the family.

"I think that's your stamp of approval." Standing she handed the kitten to the boy. Linda watched Katie with pride and thought about how grown up she was becoming.

The woman looked right into Katie's eyes.

"The very best life. I promise." Katie felt the sudden urge to hug her. The woman must have sensed it too because she drew Katie in for a very brief heartfelt hug. "The best, I promise," she whispered again.

The couple and the teenaged boy carrying the kitten in a cardboard cat carrier turned, and then they walked across the room and up the two steps to the door.

"Wait," Katie shouted. "What's his name?" The three people looked at each other smiling.

"We will call him Manuel!" said the boy.

"Bye Manuel," said Katie and Linda in unison. The door chimes jingled as they walked out. The room seemed quiet despite the hum of the many animals.

"You ok?" Linda asked tilting her head slightly.

"Yes," said Katie. "I really am."

Inside the cardboard cat carrier

Manuel dug his claws into the floor of the box in an effort to stop himself from sliding around. He could hear voices just over the sound of his pounding heart. He heard a door slam. It became very quiet. He heard another door slam. He could hear the sound of a radio and an engine running. He didn't know what all those noises were beyond the voices but there were a lot of new sounds.

He was scared. He was so scared. He scratched at the walls. He couldn't see anything except tiny beams of light coming down through the holes in the roof of his little prison. This was WORSE than the cage he'd been in for the last few months. Where were they taking him? He remembered the last time he had been in this situation. He thought about the man in the white coat. He felt a twinge of pain as he remembered going to sleep and waking up in hurting. He began to cry. His meows were high pitched and squeaky. He looked for way out. He looked to the ceiling and saw an eye peering in.

"It's ok," said a calming voice. He cried again. He cried and cried. A finger poked down through the hole and stroked him on the head. He wanted to see the people. He didn't like this dark box.

"We're almost home," said a remote voice. Manuel tried to summon his courage and be brave but his long mews seemed to be involuntary.

Suddenly, the engine noise stopped. The box jiggled. He was being moved again and tried to hold on for the ride. He tried not to imagine what was about to happen. He hoped it would be a good thing.

Light appeared above him and Manuel saw the three faces of the people he had just met. He ducked down in the box momentarily. Everything was quiet and still.

The kitten slowly put his paws up on the side of the box. His eyes scanned the upper part of the room. Suddenly he pounced out of the box. He looked around. He was in a new place. He involuntarily purred. He stopped. He listened. Something was coming around the corner. He crouched down. An enormous tabby cat crept out from behind a door. He looked very much like his roommate from the shelter.

Manuel bounded up to the enormous animal. The cat had black and brown stripes all over him which seemed to all swirl together, green eyes, a white chin and long white whiskers. "Hi!" he said with a squeak." The cat's ears went straight back, almost flat against his head.

"HCCCCCCCCCCHHHHHHH," the tabby hissed exposing two giant fangs. The kitten stepped boldly forward.

"I just wanted to..."

"HCHHHHHHHH," the cat hissed again backing up slightly. Someone shouted "Basil!" and the big cat ran away.

Manuel peeked cautiously around the door not sure what else to expect. He entered the kitchen slowly. The man, the woman and the boy watched. The kitten looked around the old farmhouse kitchen. It was absolutely gigantic compared to his little cage. He took a few more steps, exploring a little further.

Another room, he entered that room. There was big comfy furniture in that room and two great big windows for him to look out. He explored a little further. He discovered a hallway and strolled along to the stairs. He was less low to the floor at this point and seemed to be enjoying himself. Suddenly, he darted up the stairs. The old farmhouse was silent except for the sound of the kitten who was now bounding from room to room. His purr echoed through the house. Every time he exerted himself he made a small humming noise.

He darted down the stairs to find the boy sitting in a chair in the living room. He was looking at something in his hands. The kitten pounced up on his lap and pushed past the device. He got right up to the boy's face. The boy could feel the vibration of the kitten's hums and purring and laughed out loud.

"Thank you! Thank you! Thank you!" shouted the kitten. The boy did not seem to hear. "THANK YOU! THANK YOU! THANK YOU!" he shouted again even louder. The boy chuckled again but did not seem to understand.

The kitten noticed the man and the woman on the biggest piece of furniture. He leaped across the room and tried again. Jumping from lap to lap. "THANK YOU! THANK YOU! THANK YOU!" he shouted over and over but they didn't get it. "WHAT DOES MANUEL MEAN?" He asked. They seemed oblivious and just patted him on the head and smiled.

For the rest of that day and into the evening Manuel ran from room to room of the old farmhouse. He explored every crevice and found the litter box in the basement. He found his very own food bowl and water bowl and took advantage of both.

When the sun had gone down the family turned off all the lights. The woman lifted Manuel up and carried him upstairs. He snuggled right down into the big comfy bed and continued to hum and purr...and purr...and purr. Just as he was drifting off he felt a gentle thud at the end of the bed. It was dark but he could just make out the shape of the enormous tabby cat as he circled and curled up at the man's feet.

"My brother," he thought and slipped into a deep sleep and made tiny snoring noises.

CHAPTER NINETEEN

The farmhouse
Fall 2002

"Come on Dukie!" shouted the woman. "We're going for a ride!" The woman sounded very excited. Duke trotted through the farmhouse kitchen and sprung out the back door. He made a dash for the truck. The rest of little family of three followed behind him. Duke jumped at the door of the truck barking twice.

"Ok, ok," said the man wearing a Cleveland Indians hat as he opened the door.

The woman buckled the little boy into a car seat in the backseat of the truck. The man sat behind the steering wheel and the woman climbed in the other side leaving Duke in the middle at the front. The young woman leaned over to Duke and buried her face in his fur. He had something that could only be described as a mane. He was nearly a year old and had gained a lot of muscle and fat since his time lost in the country. His fur was also starting to thicken for winter. The woman took a deep inhale.

"I just love you Duke." She pulled his face toward her. Duke's bushy tail waved back and forth happily. Duke's mouth was open with his tongue hanging out. He'd never imagined what it would be like to have a family but all he knew was that right then he was the happiest he had ever been.

"Where are we taking Duke?" a high voice came from the backseat. The woman turned to her son.

"We're not taking him anywhere Honey, we're getting him a brother!" she smiled.

"Oh." The boy seemed unconcerned and looked out the window bouncing his feet against the car seat.

"Where do you want to start?" The man put the truck in gear and started down the driveway.

"Why not the pound?" she asked.

"Ok then. To the pound." The man turned the truck at the end of the driveway and headed for the county pound.

County Pound
Fall 2002

Ricky Wrigley wore black rubber Wellington boots in the back exercise yard while he played with a large bull mastiff named King. He threw a Kong ball first and then a rubber chicken. The exercise yard was quite worn and the grass struggled to keep roots in the ground. The area was penned in by chain link fence and in the corner was one small green bench. The dog was wearing himself out hurling the chicken up in the air and running back to Ricky just as Ricky would throw the Kong.

Ricky tried to fit as much exercise as he could into the short time he had with each dog in the exercise yard. This particular dog had rust colored fur and floppy ears. His snout was all black as if he'd been rooting around in some sort of soot.

"Come on boy!" called Ricky to the dog who charged toward him at the sound of his call. "Times up for now but we'll come back out after dinner," he tousled the dog's ears before slipping a slip collar around his neck. He led the dog through the backdoor of the cinder block building and closed the door behind him. He could see that a family had entered at the front lobby.

"Be right with you!" Ricky called out.

"No worries," said the man.

Ricky strolled down the hallway toward the lobby. He stood at the metal half door separating the lobby from the dogs holding the mastiff firmly.

"We're looking to add a dog to our family," said the young man in a Cleveland Indians hat. A young boy stood beside him.

"We brought our Duke!" said the little boy.

"You did?" asked Ricky. He adjusted his round wire-rimmed glasses and looked down at the boy.

"Well, we figure he came first so he'd have to approve too," said the young woman.

"That's a very good idea," Ricky said directly to the little boy as if it were solely his idea. "Age, sex, breed preference?" Ricky directed his attention to the couple.

"We're thinking about a puppy just because we have Duke, who is quite young and of course, a young child," replied the woman looking at the bull mastiff.

"We have several puppies. Let's go take a look." Ricky turned to the door.

"Where did he come from?" asked the woman looking at the young dog on the end of Ricky's leash. Ricky smiled down at this canine friend.

"Well, several days ago a man dropped this guy off. He said the dog had belonged to a friend and was homeless after his friend died suddenly. He's very friendly and it was obvious someone has spent a lot of time with him. I'm happy to say I think he has a home. A couple was in yesterday and played with him. They said they were going to go buy a crate and dog food and would be back today." Ricky turned to lead the couple back to the dogs.

"Shall we go look?" the man gestured to the woman.

"You go Honey and we'll go get Duke. Just follow your heart and meet us out at the truck and we'll get Duke's opinion." The man nodded and followed Ricky through the door.

Outside, the woman leaned against the truck holding Duke on a leash. It was a sunny fall day with just a slight chill in the air. The little boy was watching the black steel door at the side of the pound. The door opened and the man wearing the Cleveland Indians hat appeared with a small black puppy of no particular breed. The puppy appeared to be spinning like a top at the end of the leash. As they approached Duke's ears perked up but then as they came closer

Duke retreated behind the woman. The man laughed as he reached his wife and son.

"I think this little guy is full of fireworks or gunpowder or something," he chuckled. Duke was now whimpering and cowering between the woman's knees. The puppy, in an attempt to reach him wound the leash in a figure eight between the woman's feet.

"Oh my goodness!" she exclaimed. Duke was desperately attempting to escape. After several moments of this chaos nothing had changed. The puppy wasn't calming down and Duke was becoming more and more distressed. "I'm sure he's lovely for someone else but not for us," she said cautiously.

"Yeah, Duke doesn't like him!" said the little boy.

The man untangled the puppy and led the incredibly excited little dog back into the building. Several moments later he reappeared with a small hound/shepherd of some kind. He had long spindly legs and was quite tall.

"Is he a puppy?" asked the woman.

"They think he's under a year," said the man. The hound approached the truck and spotted the young boy. He growled slightly. The woman locked eyes with her husband and the man pulled back on the leash.

"Might have had a bad experience with kids." He turned pulling the dog away. "Some dogs just aren't good with kids," he said. "He'll do well for someone with older kids or no kids. Stay right there!" He called back as he reentered the pound.

Several minutes went by and the man appeared yet again with a small white and brown pup. He approached the truck. The dog looked at Duke and the boy and then away at the parking lot.

"Go ahead, bring him over," said the woman. "What is he?" she asked.

"Not sure, Ricky said part lab, part pointer of some sort. They think he's about 12 weeks. " He watched the puppy approach Duke. His tail made actual circles like a helicopter. Then the man allowed the dog to get close to his son with a tight hold on the leash. The white dog sniffed the boy's shoes and all the while his tail spun like a helicopter propeller. The dog then went back over to Duke and they nearly bumped noses. They sniffed each other's important bits. Duke sat down and the white dog turned and sat down next to him nearly shoulder to shoulder. They were each looking in either direction and looked as if they'd know each other all their lives.

"Well, look at that," whispered the man taking his baseball hat off and rubbing his head momentarily before putting it back on. He bent down and picked up the dog, cradling him belly up. The dog's paws flopped submissively. "What do you think?" he asked his family. "Duke seems to like him." he continued. He looked up from the pup at his wife. She had a little well of tears in each eye.

"Yes," she said with a lump in her throat. "Yes, he will be just fine." She turned to her son. "How about that helicopter tail?" she giggled.

"Like a chopper," said the boy.

"Chopper," the couple said it at the same time and didn't have to say one more word to know their new dog's name was Chopper. Chopper lay in the man's arms, tail spinning below him as the growing family of now five approached the cinder block building to fill out the forms.

"We're ready Rick…" the man shouted but his words caught in his throat. The woman gasped and took the hand of the little boy. There stood Ricky gently taking a very bloody, badly injured dog from an older woman.

"What's wrong?" asked the boy staring at the poor creature.

"Hit by a car," the woman replied as she carefully handed off the dog.

"Thanks Kath," Rick said quietly as if he knew the woman and this wasn't the first time this had happened. The dog was very limp.

"Is he going to die?" the boy asked.

"We'll do what we can for him," Ricky said and quickly carried the dog toward a door that said Authorized Personnel Only. "Charlotte can help you fill out the forms," his voice trailed off as he disappeared with the injured dog and the steel door slammed behind him.

A woman behind the counter held out a clipboard.

"We just need you to fill out these forms and I'll need to see some ID," she continued holding out the papers. The family of three holding Duke and the brown and white dog on a leash stood speechless as they stared at the closed door.

CHAPTER TWENTY

The old farmhouse
Late Summer 2015

The farmhouse was quiet and still except for the gentle pitter-patter of rain on the roof. . The people had all gone wherever they go all day, nearly every day. Manuel woke up and stretched his whole body across the bed. He opened his mouth and let out a big yawn. He shook his head slightly and gave his back a quick lick before slowly rising up into a sitting position. His two front paws perched at the end of the bed and he could see his reflection in the mirror. His bladder had woken him from his afternoon nap.

He looked around the room and gently hopped off the bed landing with a slight thud on the hardwood floor. He padded across the room, out the door and down the stairs. He moved cautiously as he approached the bottom of the stairs. He wasn't afraid of the big tabby cat they called "Basil" but he didn't like to be hissed at either. During the day the big cat hid under the brown recliner. He stayed hidden all day until the people came home. Manny didn't understand why the big cat was so mean. He just wanted to be friends…brothers. For weeks he had been trying to make friends but the big cat returned his affection with long hisses and tail thrashes.

Manuel trotted quietly down the hallway and slipped through the opening to the basement which housed two litter boxes. The basement was quite dark because it was raining and the sun was blocked out by all the clouds. Manuel turned the corner at the bottom of the basement stairs and his pupils widened as they adjusted to the darkness. He froze. Basil was perched in one litter box and he glared at Manuel daring him to move forward. Manuel remained frozen as he stared back. Not even a whisker moved. His green eyes fixed as he stood completely motionless. Basil glared back as if the two cats were having a stare down.

Suddenly Manuel leaped forward in one swift move. Basil hissed as he braced himself for a fight. Manuel was in the air as Basil clenched his paws exposing his sharp claws. To his surprise Manuel went right over the tabby's head and pounced on something behind him. There was a scuffle and Manuel let out a low growl and a hiss. Basil jumped out of the litter box to get a better view. Manuel had a good grip on the middle of large garter snake's slithery body. His teeth were sunk in but the snake's head and tail swung wildly. The snake was biting at the air and was getting very close to Manuel's ear when Basil instinctively pounced on the snake's throat. The snake's struggle was very brief before he went limp. Manny and Basil stood panting over the snake for a few minutes making sure it was dead.

Basil turned around and walked slowly to the bottom of the stairs. He turned and looked back at Manuel.

Manuel hopped into the litter box momentarily keeping an eye on the dead snake and then hopped out before trotting quickly past Basil and darting up the stairs. Manny ran all the way back up the stairs to the bedroom. He sprung up on the bed and groomed himself vigorously before curling up in a little ball. He stared at the doorway for a few minutes before closing his eyes to resume his daily afternoon nap.

Manny had been asleep for only a few minutes when he heard a small scuffling sound from the stairs. He opened one eye to see Basil reach the top of the staircase. He was making a low growling sound and he was dragging the dead snake. Basil looked right at Manny as he drug the snake into the center of the rug and dropped its lifeless body in the middle of the room. He made two leaps toward the bed and cleared the bench at the foot. Manny recoiled momentarily as the big cat landed hard next to him.

"Scoot over," said the tabby. Manuel scooted over a bit and Basil slipped down next to him by the pillows. Manuel thought he detected a purr.

"You might be alright kid," Basil said nodding toward the snake. "That's your kill. You should be the one to give it to them," he continued. Manuel didn't know what to say. He was just happy that the tabby was not hissing at him.

"Uh, thanks," he said quietly. The little cat didn't know where to look as he awkwardly tried to think of things to say. "I thought you didn't like me," he blurted out and immediately regretted it.

"I didn't but it's not your fault," said the bigger cat.

"Oh," said Manny searching for something to say. "I thought it might be because I'm a stray," he continued wishing he would stop talking.

"Shoot, no," said Basil with a chuckle. "Please. Stray? That's nothing,

I'm feral," he continued as if Manny knew what feral meant.

"What's that mean? What's feral?" he finally asked.

"It means I'm the son of a tomcat. I was born out in the barn and my mother moved the litter without me," he continued, his voice was low and wise.

"Why?" Manny asked.

"Could have been danger. She might not have had enough milk to feed us all..." Manny stared wide-eyed as he tried to comprehend this revelation.

"The reason doesn't matter. It happens. But here's thing, I was blind and wet and alone. It was cold and I was scared. The man saw me and rescued me. He picked me up out of the straw and carried me in his pocket," the cat said quietly. "He brought me into this house and wrapped me in a warm blanket. He and the woman fed me and washed me and made sure I was safe and warm. They love me and I love them," he was almost whispering now. "So, you see it's not that you're a stray, believe me." He looked out across the room. "That's got

nothing to do with it," he said so distantly he seemed to be thinking out loud.

"So why do you always hiss at me?" asked Manny.

Basil's gaze softened as he looked at the little gray kitten. "I'll try not to do that so much. But the rest is a story for another day. Okay?"

"Okay," said Manuel content that the cat was being a little bit nicer for the meantime. Basil stood up and abruptly jumped off the bed, trotted past the dead snake and slipped down the stairs.

The farmhouse
Summer 2007

Duke and Chopper were asleep on the kitchen floor with the little tabby cat when the woman called their names. She whistled enthusiastically and opened the door. They knew it was time to go pee. The dogs scrambled out the door and the tabby stayed behind. He didn't have very good memories of being outside and he was happy to stay in the warm house and take advantage of the never ending supply of food, water and the litter box in the basement

.

The dogs ran shoulder to shoulder in the warm summer air as they went about their routine of first bounding back to the barn together and then separating to cover all the property thoroughly. The dogs covered the whole length of the property to be sure there were no intruders or issues.

Chopper finished his side and galloped over to Duke. He feigned an inability to stop and collided into Duke's side.

"Hey!" barked Duke chuckling and ramming a shoulder into Chopper.

"Hey! Watch it!" barked Chopper even louder, and the two dogs began wrestling and playfully biting each other. They were barking and rolling around in the sunshine for some time before wearing themselves out and settling down in the warm grass together enjoying the warm breeze on the air.

"We've got it good don't we?" asked Chopper to his brother.

"We sure do," said Duke who was now upside down scratching his back on the warm ground. "We sure do," he repeated.

"Too bad Basil can't come out," said Chopper.

"He doesn't want to. He told me. He's perfectly happy in the house. He gets his thrills killing the mice in the basement. He's a cave dweller," laughed Duke as he wriggled his back all over the lawn.

Chopper's head suddenly turned to the barn and he froze.

"What?" asked Duke rolling onto his front and looking right at Chopper.

"Shhhhh," said Chopper quietly. Duke always deferred to Chopper when it came to hunting. Duke was good at keeping everyone together but Chopper was the hunter. Chopper lowered his head as he slowly stood up on all four legs. His nose was pointed at the barn.

"Follow my lead," he took one step forward. "Groundhog," he said very quietly as he ever so slowly inched forward.

The sunflowers in front of the barn moved unnaturally and Chopper's position was fixed. Duke moved a little bit to the right to deter any escape. The groundhog chewed on a big sunflower leaf as just his head emerged from the sunflower stems. He spotted Chopper, turned and spotted Duke. He was trapped. Chopper's shoulder muscles twitched as he anticipated his next move. The groundhog's teeth chattered as he stared at Chopper.

Chopper calculated, waited and then suddenly dove onto the groundhog who made a high pitched shriek. Chopper rolled and wrested with the angry animal in front of the sunflowers. Chopper pinned the groundhog down underneath him with his front paws. He was about to get him by the throat when the groundhog bit the leg closest to him causing Chopper to reel back. The groundhog saw his chance and lurched toward Chopper sinking his teeth into Chopper's throat.

Duke let out a loud bark, and pounced on the rodent's back sinking his teeth into the groundhog's rubberlike flesh. The ground hog shrieked again and let go of Chopper's throat. Duke picked the groundhog up by his back and hurled him into the air. Chopper dove forward and got the groundhog by the back of the neck. Duke growled angrily as Chopper similarly threw the groundhog up and then onto the ground. Duke went for him but just then the large rodent got his feet under him and ran, rolls of fat waddling as he managed to slip away and escape into the woods.

Duke ran to Chopper. "You ok?" Chopper was panting and covered in blood as he stared at the woods.

"I don't know. Am I?" He turned and looked at Duke. Duke leaned in to inspect his brother's throat before letting out a relieved bark. "He got your collar!" Duke said breathing a sigh of relief.

"Really?" asked Chopper trying in vain to look down at his own throat.

"Yeah Dude, you have two bucktoothed groundhog bite marks in your collar," Duke was laughing because he was so relieved.

"What about the blood?" Chopper leaned in to look Duke over. "Are you okay?" he said now greatly concerned that Duke was injured.

"Nah, it's his. I got a hold of him a little bit. He'll be sore but he'll be back to fight another day," he said.

"Whew! That was crazy!'

"I know," said Duke. "I thought you were a goner."

"Nah, I wasn't worried," laughed Chopper. "I knew you had my back bro," Chopper playfully brushed against Duke.

"Man, that was AWESOME!" exclaimed Duke as they trotted toward the house. "I can't wait to tell Basil," he shouted excitedly as they began to run full speed.

"Yeah wait 'til Basil hears this!" The two dogs chattered excitedly as they ran to the farmhouse to tell Basil about their great groundhog adventure.

CHAPTER TWENTY ONE

The farmhouse
Late summer 2015

Manuel groomed himself at the top of the stairs. It was midday and again everyone had gone out. Just the two cats remained in the house just as it was almost every day. Basil had been kinder to Manny than he was originally but Manuel could still tell something was wrong. Manny licked his back until all the fur was neatly combed in one direction. He leaned back on his backside and lifted his right rear leg up and chewed between his little pink toes.

Manuel was suddenly aware of Basil who had slinked up behind him. Basil stepped up next to Manny and sat down next to him. Their tails swung slowly and gently in unison as Basil spoke.

"Do you want to know the rest of the story?" he asked his younger brother.

"Uh, yeah I think so," said Manny cautiously.

"Come on. I'll tell you the rest." Basil slid back and turned to enter the bedroom. Manny followed. The two cats jumped up on the bed. Basil stretched out and put his paws in front of him. Manny followed suit so that they were face to face. Basil blinked slowly three times before he started. Manny's heartbeat quickened a bit.

"I've never spoken about this before okay? So be patient and if I stop in the middle and leave, just accept that I'm done talking. Okay?" he asked the little gray cat.

"Okay," said Manny.

"I used to have two brothers," sighed Basil despondently. "They were my very best friends in the whole world. One was named Duke and the other one was named Chopper," continued Basil. Manny sat quietly listening and blinking slowly. "They were both dogs."

"Dogs?"

"Yes dogs," Basil continued sounding a bit annoyed. "They were the

first things I saw when I opened my eyes after the man rescued me. They mothered me at first. They groomed and licked my fur. They cared about me. They didn't treat me like I was not any different from them. They accepted me as a brother." Basil looked around the room for a moment. "We all lived in this house for years and years. Duke slept on the landing just to make sure no one ever hurt us in the night and Chopper would kill anything moving outside. But they were gentle and fun too. They used to tell me stories and sometimes we would chase each other around the house just for fun."

Manny loved that idea and couldn't keep quiet. "That sounds great!" he blurted out.

"It was," replied Basil his head dropping a bit.

"So…" Manny said cautiously. "Where are they now?"

Basil looked right into Manuel's eyes. He didn't know if he could go on. He looked at the kitten and thought about how innocent he was. He knew

Manuel didn't have a clue about the world and he was just trying to learn. Basil summoned up all his courage and continued.

"One day Duke stopped coming upstairs. He just stopped. He slept on the kitchen floor all alone. Some nights I would stay with him. He told me his legs hurt and that he was confused. He said sometimes he couldn't hear, his eyes were cloudy and sometimes he forgot where he was."

Basil paused and swallowed hard. "One night while I was keeping him company he told me he was going on journey. He said he was very old and that he was going to have to say goodbye," Basil paused again. "He told me he was going over a bridge that would take him home. But he said it was ok because someday I would go too and we would see each other again," Basil stopped and looked at Manuel whose chin had dropped down onto his paws. His eyes were wide and sad as he looked up and listened.

"That's terrible," he said softly.

"I know," said Basil. "It is. It was. I begged him not to go but he said it was time and that he wasn't scared at all. He said he was really tired and he was ready to go home. I told him he was home. But he told me where he was going his legs wouldn't hurt and he could chase balls again and his cloudy vision would be clear. He said it would all be ok and we had a really good long cuddle that night. The next day he didn't come home. I waited and waited but he didn't come back. "

"I'm so sorry," said Manny quietly. "But, is that why you were so mad at me?" Manny was confused.

"Well, that's not the whole story," Basil continued.

"I missed Duke terribly but I still had Chopper." Basil dropped his head. "Then, not long after Duke left, one night Chopper came to me and said he was saying goodbye. I couldn't believe it was happening again!"

"Oh no. Not again," said Manuel with deep sincerity.

"Again, I begged him not to go but he said his legs wouldn't work anymore and he couldn't get outside." Basil looked at Manny inquisitively. "You know dogs poop and pee outside right?" Manny nodded. He knew from the shelter.

"He said he was going to a place where his legs would work like new. He left too and never came back."

Manny let out a long sigh.

"So, when you just popped out of that box I thought they were trying to replace my two big brothers with you," he tilted his head slightly. "No offense but you're no substitute."

"No, I'm not," said Manny quietly.

"But, you're growing on me kid,"

"Maybe I'm not a substitute for them but maybe we could still be brothers. Cat brothers."

"I'm starting to see that," said Basil. The two cats instinctively jumped down from the bed together.

"You know, I actually feel a little better for having got that off my chest," Basil chimed as they trotted down the stairs.

"Last one to the food bowl is a rotten egg," shouted Manny as he darted ahead. Basil's gate quickened as he followed behind and then slowed suddenly.

"Don't push it kid," he muttered.

CHAPTER TWENTY TWO

The farmhouse
Late summer 2016

Basil and Manuel were dozing a respectful distance from one another on the big bed. The sun shone in through the window and warmed them nicely. Manuel snored quietly and Basil lazily readjusted himself as the afternoon wore on.

Suddenly the cats were rudely awakened by a terrible commotion coming from outside the window. Manuel's eyes opened and he jumped up. He was first to reach the windowsill but Basil wasn't far behind. Manuel stared at the subject making all the commotion.

"Oh boy," Basil whispered.

Something black and white was in the back garden and it was very noisy. It was running back and forth across the deck and grassy areas. The man, the woman and the young man, who was once a boy were chasing it around and laughing joyfully.

"Is that what I think it is?" asked Manuel.

"Yep. It's exactly what you think it is. It's a puppy,'" sighed Basil.

"He sure is little. I've seen one of those at the shelter. They called it a Spaniard."

"Spaniel." Basil corrected him.

"He looks insane," said Manny staring at the excited dog.

"All puppies are insane," said Basil.

"Is he coming in here? Is he coming to live with us?" asked Manny indignantly.

"Yep," said Basil flatly as he plopped down onto the floor with a thud. "He's coming in here and he's staying forever. My advice is to just get used to it." Basil looked back at Manny as if he should follow him.

"Come on. We better go get a better look at him," Basil said with an air of sarcasm. "Dogs are ok it just looks like

this one needs a lot, and I do mean a lot of training," he sighed.

The two cats trotted shoulder to shoulder across the bedroom and then down the stairs to size up their new little brother.

"Here we go again," Basil said and Manny nodded.

"Yep, here we go again..." Manny said pretending to understand.

The end…or is it the beginning?

EPILOGUE
Winter 2030

Kate Thompson-Collins carried a bowl of popcorn into the dining room and set it down on the table between her husband, Mark and her daughter, Emily.

"Dad! Am I a hamburger?" Emily had a picture of a toothbrush on a card strapped to her head.

"No!" shouted the young man with brown curly hair.

Katie playfully tousled her husband's curly hair and knocked the Headbanz band off his head.

"Hey! What did I do?" he giggled.

"Somehow I know you're gonna cheat," Katie said winking at Emily.

"He always cheats!" Emily said laughing. Emily had long light red hair and her mother's big green eyes.

"I do not!" The man tossed a handful of popcorn in his mouth.

The family chaos continued all evening and when family game night was over and Emily was full of popcorn and root beer Katie carried her sleepy daughter up to bed. She helped her groggily brush her teeth and, she tucked Emily in and turned off the lamp. Katie made her way back downstairs and into the kitchen.

"I'll take care of all of this Hon, you just go on up to bed," said Kate's husband Mark.

"You're the best," whispered Kate, and kissed her husband on the cheek.

Kate strolled out into the living room and turned off the side table lamp. She walked over and turned off the gas that was fueling the fire in the fireplace. She stood up and put her hands on her hips and let out a sigh.

"Let's get you up to bed Twinkle," she lifted a very plump, gray cat gently from the chair. "Goodness, we need to put you on a diet my dear," she said, placing the cat on her shoulder and heading for the stairs. "But then again you are kind of an old lady so I'll cut you a break." She gently hugged Twinkle's plump belly. The cat made a little hum and then a deep purr could be heard all the way up the stairs and even as Kate entered the bedroom.

Downstairs Mark finished cleaning the kitchen and turned off the light. He stepped out into the front room and checked the front door. He turned and put one foot on the first step of the stairs and paused. He could hear that purr from all the way upstairs.

"Katie and that cat," he muttered and shook his head. He smiled and trotted up to the stairs.

"Hey, save me a spot in bed you two!" he called out playfully.

AUTHOR'S NOTES

I hope you have enjoyed reading Stray. It was a pleasure to write and all the animals you have met were based on real animals I have known or encountered in my life. *However, this is a work of fiction. Names, characters, places and incidents either are products of the author's imagination or are used fictitiously. Any resemblance to actual events or locales or persons, living or dead, is entirely coincidental.*

If you would like to share your Stray story please join our public facebook page. "Stray- Your Stories" There you can post a picture of your cherished pet and tell us your love stories. You can post in Memoriam if yours has gone over the Rainbow Bridge or tell us about the one asleep on your lap.

Please promote this book on social media so that we can help the lost. The more you share, the more we can help. You can refer people to find this book on Amazon and Kindle.

Please remember to spay and neuter. It's really important. Support your local shelters and pounds. Consider adopting a shelter pet and let's prosecute animal abuse and dog fighting to the fullest extent of the law.

A portion of the proceeds from this book will go directly to supporting our local shelters and pounds. The author picture on the back is the real "Duke" taken the day before he went on his journey home. Take good care of each other and never be afraid to love.

Suzanne DiTommaso

Made in the USA
San Bernardino, CA
17 March 2017